400+ DRIVING TEST QUESTIONS AND ANSWERS TO HELP YOU ACE YOUR EXAM WITH SUCCESS

CALIFORNIA DMV HANDBOOK 2023

Table of Contents

CHAPTER 1: Introduction to the California DMV Exam

The California DMV Exam is a written exam that evaluates your understanding of traffic rules, regulations, and safe driving practices. This introduction gives an overview of the exam structure and criteria to assist you understand what to anticipate when you sit for the test.

Exam Format:

➢ The test comprises of multiple-choice questions, where you will be provided with various possibilities and must pick the right answer.
➢ The amount of questions may vary; however, it normally runs from 36 to 46 questions.
➢ To pass the test, you must answer at least 30 or more questions correctly, depending on the total amount of questions.

Exam Content:

➢ The test covers many subjects connected to driving and traffic laws, including traffic signs, right-of-way rules, speed limits, parking restrictions, and more.

- Questions may also concentrate on defensive driving tactics, addressing emergency circumstances, and comprehending the obligations of being a driver.
- Study Materials: It is vital to study the California Driver Handbook published by the DMV. This booklet offers all the required material to prepare for the test.
- Additional study tools, such as practice tests and workbooks, might be beneficial in reinforcing your knowledge and familiarizing yourself with the exam format.

Exam criteria:

- To take the California DMV Exam, you must be at least 15 and a half years old and satisfy the criteria for getting a learner's permit or driver's license.
- Proof of identity and residence may be requested for taking the test.
- Some persons may be entitled for adjustments, such as additional time or alternate formats, if they have specific limitations.

Exam Preparation Tips:s

- Read the California Driver Handbook attentively to understand the laws and regulations.

➢ Take use of practice exams and study tools to check your knowledge and uncover areas that need more concentration.

➢ Review the handbook's summary sections and any related study aids to reinforce crucial topics.

➢ Familiarize yourself with typical traffic signs, signals, and pavement markings.

➢ Practice defensive driving tactics and comprehending right-of-way regulations.

Remember, the California DMV Exam is meant to verify that drivers have a good grasp of traffic regulations and safe driving habits. By studying the supplied materials and preparing sufficiently, you may boost your chances of passing the test on your first try. Good luck with your preparation!

Tips for studying and preparing for the exam:

Studying for the California DMV Exam needs a mix of comprehending traffic rules, regulations, and safe driving habits. Here are some recommendations to help you efficiently prepare for the exam:

➢ Read the California Driver Handbook: The manual is the key reference for preparing for the test. Read it carefully to acquaint yourself with traffic regulations, road signs, and safe driving tactics. Pay special attention to parts addressing right-of-way requirements, parking regulations, and speed limitations.

➢ Take Practice exams: Practice exams are useful for checking your knowledge and becoming acquainted with the exam style. Several internet sites provide practice exams that replicate the real DMV exam. These assessments help you discover weak areas and target your study efforts appropriately.

➢ Review Road Signs & Signals: Memorize the many kinds of traffic signs, signals, and pavement markings. Understand their meanings and how to react to them. Use flashcards or other tools to enhance your understanding of traffic signs and signals.

➢ Create a Study Schedule: Plan a study regimen that enables you to cover the topic methodically. Break down the material into digestible bits and designate specified time windows for studying each component. Consistency is crucial, so be sure to set up devoted study time every day.

➢ Study in a Quiet Environment: Find a peaceful and distraction-free location to study. Minimize interruptions and distractions to help you concentrate and recall knowledge better. Consider utilizing noise-cancelling headphones or locating a tranquil environment, such as a library.

➢ interact in Active Learning: Instead of passively reading the content, actively interact with it. Take notes, mark significant parts, and ask yourself questions to strengthen learning. Discuss the topic with a study partner or family member to better consolidate your understanding.

➢ Use Visual Aids: Utilize visual aids such as diagrams, charts, and graphics to help your grasp of complicated subjects. Visual representations may make it simpler to understand and recall knowledge.

➢ Ask explanation: If you come across any perplexing or unclear issues while studying, don't hesitate to ask explanation. Consult the California Driver Handbook, internet resources, or seek out to experienced drivers who can assist answer your concerns.

➢ Take Breaks: Studying for lengthy durations might lead to weariness and impaired retention. Take frequent pauses throughout your study sessions to rest, refresh, and assimilate the knowledge. Use this time to participate in activities that help you relax and alleviate tension.

➢ Stay Confident and Positive: Maintaining a positive mentality and believing in your abilities to accomplish is vital. Avoid becoming disheartened by tough questions or ideas. Focus on your development and believe in the work you have put into your preparation.

Remember, extensive preparation is important to passing the California DMV Exam. By following these guidelines and keeping devoted to your study schedule, you'll boost your chances of success. Best of luck on your test!

CHAPTER 2: Traffic Laws and Regulations

Understanding traffic signs, signals, and pavement markings

Understanding traffic signs, signals, and pavement markings is vital for safe and responsible driving. This section focuses on the numerous sorts of signs, signals, and markings you may see on the road. Familiarizing yourself with their terms can help you traverse the streets successfully and comply with traffic rules.

1. Road Signs:

➢ Regulatory Signs: These signs have white or red backgrounds and highlight traffic rules and regulations. Examples include stop signs, yield signs, speed restriction signs, and one-way signs.

➢ Warning Signs: These signs have yellow backgrounds and caution drivers of possible risks ahead. Examples include bends, slippery road, school zone, and deer crossing signs.

➢ Guide Signs: These signs give information about destinations, distances, and services. Examples include route signs, exit signs, and street name signs.

➢ Construction Signs: These signs are used in construction zones to convey information and cautions about temporary circumstances. Examples include diversion signs, roadwork ahead signs, and flagger ahead signs.

➢ Emergency Signs: These signs are intended to advise cars during crises, such as evacuation routes or regions with limited access.

2. Traffic Signals:

➢ Red Light: Requires automobiles to come to a full stop before the junction line or crosswalk.

➢ Green Light: Permits automobiles to continue if the junction is clear.

➢ Yellow Light: Warns vehicles that the signal is about to change to red and suggests that they should prepare to stop safely if they can do so.

➢ Flashing Signals: Used in many scenarios, such as flashing red lights at stop signs or pedestrian crosswalks, cautioning cars to continue with care.

3. Pavement Markings:

➢ Lane Markings: Solid lines indicate no lane changes, whereas dotted lines enable lane changes if safe. Yellow lines divide traffic driving in opposing directions, while white lines separate vehicles traveling in the same direction.

> ➤ Crosswalks: Marked with strong white lines to indicate where pedestrians should cross the road.

> ➤ Stop Lines: Solid white lines positioned before junctions, indicating where cars should stop when confronted with a stop sign or traffic signal.

> ➤ Arrows: Used to denote certain driving operations, such as turn lanes or directions at junctions.

> ➤ Symbols and Words: Painted on the road to convey extra information, such as disability parking spots, bike lanes, or bus-only lanes.

It is vital to comprehend and obey the directions communicated by traffic signs, signals, and pavement markings. Ignoring or misinterpreting these might lead to driving tickets or accidents. Regularly reread the California Driver Handbook to reinforce your understanding of these vital parts of traffic rules and regulations.

Remember, always be vigilant to the road and drive defensively, taking into consideration the information offered by signs, signals, and pavement markings. Safe and responsible driving needs continual awareness of your surroundings and compliance with traffic regulations.

Right-of-way regulations and procedures

Right-of-way regulations and procedures are crucial to ensuring safe and orderly traffic movement. Understanding and appropriately executing these principles is vital for reducing accidents and promoting smooth interactions between cars, pedestrians, and other road users. Here's an outline of right-of-way regulations and procedures:

1. General Right-of-Way Rules:

➢ give: When approaching a junction or merging area, give the right-of-way to other cars, pedestrians, or cyclists already at the intersection or merging lane.

➢ Four-Way Stops: At a junction with stop signs for all incoming directions, the vehicle that arrives first has the right-of-way. If numerous cars arrive simultaneously, the vehicle on the right has the right-of-way.

➢ Uncontrolled junctions: At junctions without traffic signs or signals, surrender the right-of-way to any vehicle already in the intersection or approaching from the right.

➢ Emergency Vehicles: When emergency vehicles (with lights and sirens) approach, give the right-of-way by moving to the right and halting until they pass.

2. Pedestrian Right-of-Way:

➤ Crosswalks: Pedestrians have the right-of-way at marked or unmarked crosswalks. Drivers must yield to pedestrians in or approaching the crossing.

➤ Pedestrian Signals: Obey pedestrian signals at junctions. If the "Walk" signal is shown, pedestrians have the right-of-way to cross in the stated direction.

3. Turning Right-of-Way:

Right Only

➤ Right Turns: When making a right turn at a junction, surrender the right-of-way to pedestrians, cyclists, and vehicles already at the intersection or coming from the opposite direction.

➤ Red Lights: In most circumstances, right turns on red are permitted unless forbidden by signage. However, yield to pedestrians and other vehicles having the right-of-way before advancing.

4. Left Turn and U-turn Right-of-Way:

Left Only

➤ Left Turns: When making a left turn, defer to incoming vehicles, including bicycles and pedestrians. Proceed with the turn only when it is safe and there is no competing traffic.

➢ U-turns: U-turns are normally permitted unless banned by signage. Yield to incoming vehicles and pedestrians before making a U-turn.

5. Special Situations:

➢ Yielding to Bicycles: Bicycles on the roads have the same rights and obligations as motor vehicles. Yield to bicycles when appropriate, such as when they are in bike lanes or crossing junctions.

➢ Yielding to Transit Vehicles: When a transit vehicle (bus, streetcar, or trolley) announces its purpose to re-enter traffic, give the right-of-way and enable it to join.

Understanding and following right-of-way regulations helps avoid accidents and encourages safe interactions amongst road users. It is vital to be aware, study the conduct of other road users, and surrender when appropriate. Familiarize yourself with the precise right-of-way regulations provided in the California Driver Handbook and always emphasize safety on the road.

Speed restrictions, passing regulations, and lane use

Speed restrictions, passing regulations, and lane use are vital parts of safe and responsible driving. Adhering to these guidelines helps preserve orderly traffic flow and decreases the chance of accidents. Here's a summary of speed restrictions, passing regulations, and lane use guidelines:

1. Speed Limits:

➢ Speed restrictions are intended to improve safety and provide a reasonable and sensible speed for varying road conditions.

➢ Always follow posted speed limit signs. Speed restrictions might vary based on the kind of road, location, and surrounding factors.

➢ Adjust your speed as required to handle severe weather conditions, heavy traffic, or other risks.

➢ Remember that speed restrictions are maximum limitations, and you should drive at a speed that is safe and acceptable for the present circumstances.

2. Passing Rules:

Right Only

➢ Before passing another vehicle, be sure it is legal and safe to do so.

➢ Only pass when there is a dotted or broken line on your side of the highway, signaling that it is safe to cross into the oncoming lane.

➢ Check your blind areas, announce your purpose, then accelerate to a safe passing speed.

➢ Maintain a safe distance from the car you are passing, and do not return to your lane until you can see the past vehicle in your rearview mirror.

➢ Do not exceed the speed limit when passing, and always yield to any cars or pedestrians already in the lane you intend to enter.

3. Lane Usage:

➢ Follow lane markings and signage indicating the proper usage of each lane.

➢ Keep to the right unless passing or ready to make a left turn.

➢ On multi-lane roadways, utilize the left lane for passing or quicker traffic and the right lane for slower speeds or quitting the route.

➢ Avoid weaving in and out of lanes excessively, since it may be harmful and interrupt the flow of traffic.

➢ Use your turn signals to indicate lane changes and enable other drivers to anticipate your movements.

4. Special Considerations:

➢ Construction Zones: Reduce your speed and observe any posted signs or directives from employees. Be prepared for lane closures and changes in travel patterns.

➢ School Zones: Observe lower speed restrictions and take care while children are around. Be prepared to stop for school buses picking up or dropping off youngsters.

Remember, it is vital to always drive at a safe and suitable pace, respect passing restrictions, and utilize lanes appropriately. Adhering to these rules leads to safer roads and a more efficient traffic flow. Familiarize yourself with precise speed limits, passing restrictions, and lane use requirements specified in the California Driver Handbook, and always prioritize the safety of yourself and others on the road.

School zones and pedestrian safety

School zones and pedestrian safety are key concerns for drivers to safeguard the well-being of children and other walkers in and around school locations. Understanding the regulations and taking required steps may help avoid accidents and promote safer surroundings. Here's an outline of school zones and pedestrian safety guidelines:

1. School Zones:

➢ School Zone Signs: School zones are designated with particular signs indicating lower speed restrictions and the hours when they are in place. Be vigilant for these indications and alter you're driving appropriately.

➢ Reduced Speed restrictions: School zones often have reduced speed restrictions, commonly 15 to 25 mph, to safeguard the safety of kids and pedestrians. Adhere to these lower speed restrictions while travelling through school zones.

➢ Flashing Lights: Some school zones are equipped with flashing lights to notify cars of the decreased speed restrictions. When the lights are flashing, lower your speed appropriately.

➢ Crossing Guards: Pay attention to crossing guards who help pedestrians in safely crossing the road. Follow their directions and yield to people they are assisting to cross.

2. Pedestrian Safety:

➢ Crosswalks: Be watchful for designated crosswalks near schools and yield to pedestrians who are walking or waiting to cross. Never block or park in a crosswalk.

➢ School Buses: Stop for school buses that are loading or unloading youngsters. Observe the "STOP" arm and flashing red lights on the bus, since this signals that minors are boarding or departing the bus.

➢ surrender to Pedestrians: Always surrender the right-of-way to pedestrians, especially near schools or at authorized crosswalks. Be patient and give them ample time to safely cross the road.

➢ Scan for youngsters: Keep a vigilant eye on youngsters, since they may be more unpredictable around school settings. Be prepared to respond and slow down if required.

➢ Distracted Driving: Avoid distractions such as using mobile devices or eating while driving, since these might divert your attention from pedestrians and other road users.

3. Additional Safety Measures:

➢ Safe Parking: Park in specified places and prevent double parking or obstructing visibility near schools. This enables good sightlines for both cars and pedestrians.

➢ Respect School rules: Familiarize yourself with any extra school rules governing drop-off and pick-up procedures.

Follow these rules to ensure a safe and controlled flow of traffic.

➢ Stay Informed: Keep informed with local school schedules, events, and road closures that may alter travel patterns around schools.

Remember, school zones demand additional care and attention from drivers. By respecting lower speed restrictions, being watchful for pedestrians, and following the directions of crossing guards and school buses, you contribute to the safety and well-being of children and other pedestrians in school zones. Always prioritize the safety of pedestrians and practice patience and vigilance while driving near schools.

Parking laws and limitations

Parking laws and limits serve a significant role in maintaining controlled traffic flow and assuring the availability of parking spots for all vehicles. Understanding and sticking to these standards is vital to prevent parking penalties and contribute to a safe and efficient parking environment. Here's an outline of parking laws and restrictions:

1. No Parking Zones:

➢ No Parking Signs: Pay heed to posted signs designating places where parking is absolutely forbidden. These zones are often identified with signs that openly proclaim "No Parking" or show particular limitations such as "No Parking Anytime" or "No Parking during specified hours."

➢ Fire Hydrants: Do not park within a set distance, generally 15 feet, of fire hydrants. This enables simple access for firemen in case of emergency.

2. Handicapped Parking:

➢ disability Parking places: Designated parking places for those with disabilities are designated with the International Symbol of Access and are allocated only for cars carrying a valid disability parking permit or license plate.

➢ Accessibility: These areas are positioned near building entrances or other amenities to allow easy access for those with impairments. Unauthorized parking in these areas may result in substantial fines and penalties.

3. Loading Zones:

➢ Loading and Unloading: Loading zones are designated places for temporary parking to ease the loading and unloading of products or people. Typically, these places are identified with signage and have particular time limitations. Use these zones exclusively for their intended purposes and during the time constraints mentioned.

4. Time-Limited Parking:

➢ Metered Parking: Parking meters demand payment for a defined duration. Park solely within the time limitations shown on the meter and ensure that your car is relocated before the time ends.

➢ Timed Parking Zones: Some places may have timed parking limitations, such as "2-hour parking" or "No Parking 7 AM to 6 PM." Adhere to these limits to ensure equitable access to parking for other cars.

5. Residential Parking:

➢ Permit Parking: In some residential neighborhoods, permits may be needed to park on the street. These permits are often granted to inhabitants of that region to assure parking availability near their residences. Non-permit holders risk obtaining tickets or being towed.

6. Additional Parking Regulations:

➢ Parking in Designated spots: Park strictly inside designated parking spots and avoid infringing on nearby spaces. This optimizes the utilization of available parking places and reduces disturbance to other cars.

➢ Prohibited locations: Do not park in locations such as intersections, crosswalks, bus stops, or bike lanes, since they hinder traffic and pose safety issues.

➢ Parking Structure/Garage Rules: Follow any stated rules inside parking structures or garages, including reserved spots, height limitations, or time limits.

Always be aware of and observe local parking rules and limits. Failure to comply with parking restrictions may result in fines, towing, or other consequences. Remember, good parking habits help to a better traffic flow and provide equitable access to parking for all vehicles.

DUI (Driving Under the Influence) laws and punishments

DUI (Driving Under the Influence) rules and penalties are in place to discourage and address the hazardous conduct of driving a vehicle while impaired by alcohol or drugs. These regulations attempt to preserve the safety of drivers, passengers, and pedestrians. Understanding DUI laws and the accompanying consequences is vital for fostering responsible and sober driving. Here's an outline of DUI rules and penalties:

1. Blood Alcohol Concentration (BAC) Limits:
➢ Legal BAC Limit: In most places, including California, the legal BAC limit for drivers aged 21 and above is 0.08%. If

your BAC is at or over this level, you are deemed legally impaired.

➢ Zero Tolerance for Underage Drivers: For drivers under the age of 21, there is a zero-tolerance policy regarding alcohol use while driving. Any detectable level of alcohol in their system might result in fines.

2. Penalties for DUI:

➢ License Suspension: A DUI conviction often leads in a suspension of driving privileges. The duration of the suspension may vary dependent on criteria such as past convictions and BAC level.

➢ penalties: DUI infractions generally come with significant penalties. The sum might change based on the exact circumstances, such as past convictions or aggravating situations.

➢ Ignition Interlock Device (IID): In certain situations, persons convicted of DUI may be obliged to install an IID in their car. This gadget monitors BAC and prohibits the car from starting if alcohol is found.

➢ Probation: DUI offenders may be put on probation, requiring frequent check-ins with a probation officer and adherence to particular requirements, such as required alcohol education programs.

➢ Jail Time: DUI convictions may result in jail or prison terms, particularly for repeat crimes or situations involving significant harm or fatality.

3. Enhanced Penalties:

➢ Aggravating Factors: Certain conditions may lead to heightened penalties, including as having a high BAC level, causing harm or death, driving with a suspended license, or having past DUI convictions.

➢ Felony DUI: Under specified conditions, like as numerous DUI convictions within a set time or causing significant harm or death, a DUI crime may be prosecuted as a felony, leading to more severe penalties.

4. Legal Process:

➢ DUI Arrest: If a law enforcement officer suspects impairment, they may undertake field sobriety tests, breathalyzer testing, or blood tests to ascertain BAC level.

➢ Legal Representation: It is crucial to speak with an attorney skilled in DUI matters if you are charged with a DUI crime. They can help you through the legal procedure and safeguard your rights.

5. Public Safety Implications:

➢ Education and Awareness: DUI laws are enforced to dissuade people from driving under the influence and to promote public awareness about the risks of impaired driving.

➤ Ride-Sharing and Alternative transit: Utilize ride-sharing services, public transit, or designate a sober driver to guarantee a safe and responsible manner to travel if you have ingested alcohol or drugs.

➤ It is crucial to prioritize the safety of yourself and others by never driving under the influence of alcohol or drugs. Familiarize yourself with unique DUI laws and penalties in your area and take proactive actions to avoid intoxicated driving. By making smart decisions, you contribute to a safer driving environment for everyone.

CHAPTER 3: Roadway Safety and Defensive Driving

Defensive driving techniques

Defensive driving practices are vital for preserving highway safety and lowering the chance of accidents. These tactics entail proactive measures and a heightened degree of awareness to anticipate and react to possible threats. By practicing defensive driving, you can safeguard yourself, your passengers, and other road users. Here are some fundamental defensive driving techniques:

1. Stay Alert and Focused:
   - Maintain concentrate on the road and prevent distractions such as mobile phones, eating, or other activities that divert your attention away from driving.
   - Scan the road ahead, continually monitoring your mirrors, blind areas, and the activities of other drivers.
   - Be prepared for unforeseen scenarios and anticipate possible risks.
2. Maintain a Safe Following gap:
   - Keep a safe gap between your car and the vehicle ahead. The suggested minimum following distance is three seconds under typical driving circumstances.

➢ Increase your following distance amid severe weather conditions, heavy traffic, or while driving at greater speeds.

➢ This gap offers you adequate time to respond and stop safely if the car in front suddenly slows down or stops.

3. Avoid Aggressive Driving actions:

➢ Control your emotions and avoid aggressive actions such as tailgating, excessive speeding, or cutting off other cars.

➢ Be patient and forgiving of other drivers' errors or habits that may anger you.

➢ Yield the right-of-way when required and state your intentions properly to communicate with other cars.

4. Observe and Follow Traffic Laws:

➢ Adhere to established speed restrictions and vary your speed according to road and weather conditions.

➢ Stop at red lights and stop signs, cede the right-of-way where needed, and obey all traffic signals and signs.

➢ Use your turn signals to indicate lane changes and turns, enabling other drivers to anticipate your movements.

5. Be Cautious at junctions:

➢ Approach junctions with caution, even when you have the right-of-way.

➢ Look for suspected red light runners or cars making quick corners.

➢ Check for pedestrians and bikers crossing the junction, and yield to them as appropriate.

6. Prepare for Potential risks:

➢ Scan the road for potential risks such as pedestrians, bicycles, debris, or animals.

➢ Be attentive of the behavior of other drivers and anticipate any possible errors.

➢ Keep a watch on the road ahead for any potential construction zones, potholes, or other impediments.

7. Stay Sober and Avoid Fatigue:

➢ Never drive under the influence of alcohol, drugs, or medicines that affect your ability to drive safely.

➢ Get adequate rest before starting on a lengthy travel to avoid sleepy driving.

Remember, defensive driving is about being proactive, vigilant, and prepared for any circumstance on the road. By implementing these strategies, you contribute to a safer driving environment for yourself and others. Stay cautious, respect traffic regulations, and prioritize the safety of everyone on the road.

Managing space and following distances

Managing spacing and following distances is a crucial part of defensive driving. It entails keeping a safe gap between your car and the vehicle ahead, enabling you ample time to react and maneuver properly. By managing space efficiently, you may lower the chance of crashes and have more control over your car. Here are some recommendations for controlling space and following distances:

1. Following Distance:

➢ Maintain a safe following distance from the car in front of you. The suggested minimum following distance is three seconds under typical driving circumstances.

➢ To calculate the following distance, pick a fixed item on the road, such as a sign or a tree. When the car ahead passes that item, count "one thousand one, one thousand two, one thousand three." If you approach the item before finishing the count, you are following too closely and should increase your following distance.

➢ Increase your following distance in severe weather conditions, heavy traffic, or while driving at greater speeds. This gives for more response time and braking distance.

2. Space Cushion:

➢ Maintain a space cushion surrounding your car. This refers to the area of vacant space that you should have on all sides of your vehicle.

➢ Keep adequate distance on your sides to prevent colliding with other cars or objects if they abruptly swerve or change lanes.

➢ Leave additional distance in front of your car to establish a buffer zone that allows for safe braking and responsiveness to unexpected stops by the vehicle ahead.

3. Lane Positioning:

➢ Position your car adequately inside the lane to generate more space and boost your visibility.

➢ Stay centered in your lane, providing space on both sides in case you need to navigate around hazards or other cars.

➢ Maintain a safe distance from parked automobiles to prevent crashes with opening doors or people entering or departing vehicles.

4. Anticipate and React:

➢ Stay attentive and continually check the road ahead for possible dangers, such as unexpected stops, road debris, or pedestrians.

➢ Anticipate the activities of other drivers and be prepared to respond appropriately. This includes indicating your intentions, changing lanes safely, and altering your speed as appropriate.

5. Adjust for Road Conditions:

➢ Adapt your following distance and spacing management depending on road conditions, such as wet or ice roads.

➢ Reduce your speed and increase your following distance while driving in inclement weather or on poorly maintained roads.

Remember, regulating spacing and following distances is vital for preserving safety on the road. By providing appropriate distance between your car and others, you have more time to respond to possible risks and may prevent crashes. Practice these strategies regularly to produce a safer driving experience for yourself and others.

Identifying and reacting to dangerous conditions

Identifying and reacting to dangerous circumstances is a vital ability for safe driving. Being able to spot possible threats on the road and taking proper action may help avoid accidents and secure your safety. Here are some suggestions for detecting and reacting to dangerous conditions:

1. Poor Weather Conditions:

➤ Rain, snow, fog, or ice may drastically impair road conditions. Slow down and increase your following distance to compensate for poor traction and visibility.

➤ Use windshield wipers, defrosters, and headlights as required to increase visibility.

➤ Be wary about hydroplaning on wet roads by lowering your speed and avoiding abrupt braking or steering motions.

2. Reduced Visibility:

➤ In situations such as heavy rain, fog, or dust storms, visibility may be severely hampered. Use your headlights and fog lights (if appropriate) to make yourself more apparent to others.

➤ Reduce your speed and increase your following distance to have more time to respond to unexpected obstructions or stopping traffic.

➤ Avoid using high lights in foggy circumstances, as they might reflect back and hamper your sight more.

3. Construction Zones:

➤ Slow down while approaching construction zones and respect any stated speed restrictions or directions from flaggers and road signage.

➤ Be prepared for narrower lanes, lane movements, and uneven road conditions.

➤ Watch out for construction workers and equipment, and allow them adequate room while going by.

4. Unpredictable Road Users:

➤ Be wary of pedestrians, cyclists, and motorcyclists who may behave unexpectedly or be less visible than other vehicles.

➤ Yield the right-of-way to pedestrians at crosswalks and be careful of sharing the road with vulnerable road users.

➤ Check your blind zones and use your turn signals while changing lanes or making changes to guarantee the safety of persons around you.

➤ Wildlife: In regions with known wildlife crossings, such as rural or forested areas, observe for signs suggesting animal crossings.

➤ Reduce your speed and take care, particularly at dawn, dusk, and overnight hours when animals are more active.

➤ If an animal is crossing the road, slow down and prevent rapid movements or swerving that might result in loss of control.

➤ Emergency Vehicles: When you see or hear emergency vehicles with flashing lights or sirens, carefully move to the right side of the road and stop.

➤ Provide ample room for emergency vehicles to pass and avoid blocking crossings or hindering their route.

5. Distracted or Impaired Drivers:

➢ Be aware for drivers who may be distracted, intoxicated, or showing unpredictable behavior.

➢ Maintain a safe distance from such drivers and report any unsafe conduct to local authorities if required.

➢ Avoid distractions yourself and keep attentive on the road at all times.

It's vital to keep aware and adjust your driving behavior to the unique situations you face. By being aware of possible dangers and behaving accordingly, you may limit risks and contribute to safer roads for yourself and others. Always prioritize your safety and the safety of others around you while detecting and reacting to dangerous circumstances.

Sharing the road with other cars, bikes, and pedestrians

Sharing the road with other cars, bikes, and pedestrians is crucial for enhancing safety and maintaining a pleasant traffic environment. Respecting the rights and space of all road users is vital to avoid accidents and maintain everyone's well-being. Here are some rules for sharing the road effectively:

1. Awareness and Communication:

➤ Stay vigilant and continually monitor the road for other cars, bikes, and pedestrians.

➤ Use your mirrors and check blind areas before changing lanes, merging, or making turns.

➤ Signal your goals in advance to express your activities to others.

2. Give Cyclists and Pedestrians Space:

➤ When passing bicycles, keep a safe gap of at least three feet (roughly one meter) to allow for their safety and mobility.

➤ Be patient and wait for a safe chance to pass bikes, taking into mind approaching traffic.

➤ Yield to pedestrians at crosswalks and be prepared to stop if someone is crossing the road.

3. Be Mindful of Bike Lanes and Shared Paths:

➤ Respect designated bike lanes and shared routes. Avoid driving or parking in these places, since they are especially allocated for bikes and pedestrians.

➤ When crossing bike lanes or shared pathways, yield to cyclists and pedestrians and verify it is safe to advance.

➤ Use Caution at Intersections: Intersections are high-risk zones. Pay special attention to traffic lights, signage, and the right-of-way laws.

➢ Look for people crossing the road and yield to them when required.

➢ Check for bicycles and allow them room while making turns or changing lanes.

4. Be Patient and Tolerant:

➢ Traffic congestion and slower-moving automobiles are prevalent on the road. Practice patience and avoid aggressive behaviour.

➢ Respect the pace and ability of bikes and slower vehicles. Only pass when it is safe to do so, allowing adequate distance between your car and theirs.

5. Watch for Vulnerable Road Users:

➢ Children, older adults, and those with impairments may have restricted mobility or be less attentive of traffic. Be extremely careful around them and allow them adequate space and time to cross the road.

6. Avoid Distracted Driving:

➢ Keep your attention focused on the road and avoid distractions such as mobile devices or other activities that pull your concentration away from driving.

➢ Do not use your phone or indulge in other distracting habits while driving.

Remember, sharing the road is a shared duty. By being thoughtful, patient, and attentive, you contribute to a safer and more cooperative driving environment. Treat all road users with respect and prioritize their safety as well as your own. Together, we can create a more peaceful and safe road-sharing experience.

Handling emergency circumstances and accidents

Handling emergency circumstances and accidents on the road demands rapid thought, serenity, and adherence to correct standards. Being prepared and understanding how to react may help limit future damage and secure the safety of people involved. Here are some principles for addressing emergency situations and accidents:

1. Stay Calm:
➢ Take a deep breath and try to stay calm. Panic might hamper your capacity to make sensible judgments and appraise the situation appropriately.
2. Ensure Safety:
➢ If feasible, transfer your car to a safe spot away from traffic to avoid future accidents or risks.
➢ Activate your warning lights to notify other vehicles of the emergency situation.
3. Check for Injuries:

➢ Assess yourself and those involved in the accident for injuries. If someone is harmed, contact for emergency aid immediately.

4. Contact Authorities:

➢ Dial the emergency services number (such as 911 in the United States) to report the accident and seek essential aid.

➢ Provide precise and thorough information regarding the location, number of cars involved, and any injuries.

5. Exchange Information:

➢ Exchange contact, insurance, and vehicle information with the other parties involved in the collision. This contains names, phone numbers, addresses, and insurance policy data.

➢ If there are witnesses, get their contact information as well, since their testimony may be important during insurance claims or legal actions.

6. Document the Accident:

Take photographs of the accident site, including the location of cars, damage, and other important facts. This paperwork may aid with insurance claims and investigations.

If necessary, make a note of the weather conditions, road conditions, and any other circumstances that may have contributed to the accident.

➢ Cooperate with Authorities: Follow the directions of law enforcement authorities and emergency personnel. Provide correct information and participate completely with their inquiries.

➢ If requested, make a statement regarding the collision, but be careful about admitting culpability or commenting on the reason. Stick to the facts as you know them.

➢ Notify Your Insurance Company: Contact your insurance company as soon as possible to report the accident and commence the claims procedure. Provide them with all the essential facts and paperwork.

➢ Seek Medical assistance: Even if you don't first feel wounded, it's crucial to seek medical assistance following an accident. Some injuries may not be immediately obvious, and a medical assessment may help detect and manage any underlying concerns.

➢ Follow Legal and Insurance Procedures: Familiarize yourself with the legal and insurance requirements relevant to your area. Adhere to any deadlines for reporting the accident or submitting claims.

Remember, prioritizing safety and following right protocols is vital in emergency circumstances and accidents. By maintaining cool, seeking aid, and collaborating with authorities, you may help guarantee the well-being of everybody involved and manage the aftermath of the event more efficiently.

CHAPTER 4: Vehicle Operations and Maintenance

Vehicle controls and instrumentation

Understanding the different controls and instruments in your car is vital for safe and successful vehicle operation. Familiarizing yourself with these components can help you drive your car effectively and adapt to diverse driving circumstances. Here are some typical car controls and instruments:

1. Steering Wheel:
   ➢ The steering wheel enables you to control the direction of your vehicle. Use both hands to retain control and make smooth, gentle bends.
   ➢ Adjust the steering wheel's position to a comfortable and ergonomic position that gives a good view of the instrument panel and road.
2. Accelerator Pedal:
   ➢ The accelerator pedal, normally positioned on the right side of the footwell, regulates the speed of the vehicle. Gradually push down on the pedal to accelerate and release it to decelerate or maintain pace.
3. Brake Pedal:

➢ The brake pedal, placed to the left of the accelerator pedal, is used to slow down or stop the vehicle. Apply strong, progressive pressure to bring the car to a smooth stop. In emergency circumstances, use hard, steady pressure for maximum braking force.

4. Clutch Pedal (Manual Transmission):

➢ In automobiles equipped with manual gearboxes, the clutch pedal is used to engage and disengage the engine from the transmission. Pressing the clutch pedal helps you to transfer gears effortlessly.

5. Gearshift (Manual and Automatic Transmissions):

➢ The gearshift enables you to pick the proper gear for your vehicle's speed and driving circumstances. In manual transmissions, change gears by moving the gearshift into the correct gear slot. In automatic transmissions, utilize the gearshift to choose between park (P), reverse ®, neutral (N), drive (D), and other gear modes as required.

6. Speedometer:

➢ The speedometer indicates the current speed of your car. It helps you maintain a safe and legal speed limit while driving.

7. Tachometer (Manual Transmission):

➢ The tachometer, featured in automobiles with manual gearboxes, indicates the engine's revolutions per minute

(RPM). It helps you monitor engine speed and pick the proper gear for best performance.

8. Fuel Gauge:

➢ The fuel gauge reveals the quantity of petrol left in your vehicle's fuel tank. It lets you check your gasoline level and prepare for refilling.

9. Temperature Gauge:

➢ The temperature gauge indicates the engine's operating temperature. It helps you monitor the engine's cooling system and identify any possible overheating concerns.

10. Oil Pressure Gauge:

➢ The oil pressure gauge gauges the oil pressure in the engine. It warns you to any anomalies in the oil circulation, which might signal a fault with the engine's lubricating system.

11. Turn Signal Controls:

➢ Use the turn signal settings to express your desire to change lanes or make a turn. Activate the proper turn signal by pulling the lever up or down, depending on the direction you wish to indicate.

12. Headlights and Wipers Controls:

➢ Operate the headlights to brighten the road ahead and boost visibility during low-light circumstances. Adjust the intensity of the headlights with the headlight control switch.

➢ Control the windshield wipers to remove rain, snow, or debris from the windshield. Adjust the wiper speed depending on the severity of precipitation.

It's crucial to study your car's owner's handbook for specific information on the controls and instruments in your particular vehicle model. Understanding and utilizing these settings correctly can improve your driving experience and guarantee a safer travel.

Proper vehicle placement and steering procedures

Proper vehicle placement and steering skills are vital for keeping control and navigating safely on the road. By learning and adopting these tactics, you may enhance your vehicle's handling and decrease the chance of accidents. Here are some suggestions for optimal vehicle posture and steering:

1. Lane Positioning:
➢ Position your vehicle inside the lane to enhance visibility and maintain a safe distance from other cars and objects.
➢ Stay centered inside your lane, avoiding straying too near to the lane markings on either side.
➢ Adjust your position as required to fit road circumstances, such as avoiding dangers or making turns.
2. Following Distance:

- Maintain a safe following distance between your car and the vehicle ahead. This offers you ample time to respond to rapid changes in traffic or road conditions.

- Use the "two-second rule" as a basic guideline. Choose a fixed item on the road and ensure that you have at least two seconds of time between when the car ahead passes the object and when your vehicle passes it.

3. Steering Techniques:

- Use a hand-over-hand or push-pull steering style for smooth and controlled bends.

- For heavier steering inputs, such as during parking maneuvers or rapid bends, employ hand-over-hand steering. This includes crossing your hands over each other on the steering wheel while keeping a tight hold.

- For modest modifications while traveling at greater speeds, employ the push-pull approach. Place your hands on opposing sides of the steering wheel and push or pull with your hands to spin the wheel.

4. Turning:

- Signal your desire to turn in advance using your vehicle's turn signal. This informs other road users of your planned move.

- Slow down before approaching a turn to provide stability and control.

➢ Follow the designated turning lane and position your car adequately inside the lane.

➢ Maintain a consistent pace throughout the turn and accelerate smoothly as you leave the corner.

5. Changing Lanes:

➢ Check your mirrors and blind areas before changing lanes to verify it is safe to do so.

➢ Signal your desire to change lanes in advance to alert other vehicles.

➢ Gradually steer towards the intended lane, keeping a smooth and controlled movement.

6. Adjusting to Road Conditions:

➢ Adapt your placement and steering tactics to meet changing road conditions, such as bends, inclines, or slick surfaces.

➢ Reduce your speed and take additional care when encountering dangerous conditions like rain, snow, or ice.

➢ retain a strong hold on the steering wheel to retain control in tough situations.

7. Parking:

➢ When parking, place your car inside the assigned parking area while giving ample room for surrounding vehicles.

➢ Use your mirrors and tilt your head to look for any impediments or pedestrians before navigating into or out of a parking place.

➢ Follow any parking laws, such as parking inside defined lines or respecting time limitations.

Remember to use these tactics often to create healthy habits and strengthen your driving abilities. Pay attention to your surroundings, anticipate changes in traffic or road conditions, and make smooth and deliberate adjustments to your vehicle's position and steering. By doing so, you may drive with confidence and contribute to safer road conditions for yourself and others.

Accelerating, braking, and signaling

Accelerating, braking, and signaling are key parts of vehicle operation that contribute to safe and efficient driving. By understanding these skills, you may traverse the road with confidence and express your intentions to other road users. Here are some rules for accelerating, braking, and signaling:

1. Accelerating:

➢ Apply steady pressure on the accelerator pedal to steadily raise your vehicle's speed.

➢ Avoid quick acceleration, since it may cause loss of traction or lead to loss of control.

➢ Adjust your acceleration depending on traffic, road conditions, and stated speed restrictions.

➢ When merging into highways or joining traffic, accelerate to match the flow of traffic while keeping a safe distance from other cars.

2. Braking:

➢ Apply the brakes gently and steadily to slow down or stop your car.

➢ Use firm, but not excessive, pressure on the brake pedal for efficient braking.

➢ Anticipate the need to slow down or halt by analyzing traffic patterns and road conditions.

➢ Modulate the brake pressure to minimize sudden stops or skidding, particularly on slick ground.

➢ Use the right braking strategy for your vehicle, such as pumping the brakes in cars without anti-lock braking systems (ABS) or exerting consistent pressure in vehicles with ABS.

3. Signaling:

➢ Use your vehicle's turn signals to announce your desire to turn or change lanes.

➢ Activate the turn signal in advance of your planned move to give other vehicles enough warning.

➢ Check your vehicle's turn signals often to verify they are operating correctly.

➢ Make careful to deactivate your turn signal after finishing the move to minimize confusion for other road users.

➢ Use hand signals in the case of a faulty or non-operational turn signal.

4. Signal Timing:

➢ Signal your intention to turn or change lanes with adequate time to enable other drivers to respond and alter their driving appropriately.

➢ Signal at least 100 feet (30 meters) before your planned turn or lane change on ordinary roadways. On highways, indicate at least five seconds before changing lanes.

5. Use of Brake Lights:

➢ Brake lights are automatically engaged when you press the brakes. They signal to traffic behind you that you are slowing down or coming to a halt.

➢ Make sure your brake lights are operating correctly, since they are vital for signaling your actions to other drivers.

➢ Avoid needless or sudden braking, since it might startle cars behind you and increase the chance of rear-end incidents.

Remember, smooth acceleration and braking, together with clear and timely signals, promote safe and predictable driving. Consistently practice these skills and maintain your vehicle's signals and brakes to guarantee maximum operation. By doing so, you contribute to a safer and more efficient driving experience for yourself and others on the road.

Changing lanes and making turns

Changing lanes and performing turns are regular operations while driving that need appropriate execution to maintain safety and efficiency on the road. Here are some recommendations for changing lanes and making turns:

1. Changing Lanes:
   - Check Your Mirrors: Before changing lanes, check your rearview mirror and side mirrors to evaluate the traffic condition behind you.
   - Use Your Turn Signal: Activate your turn signal to express your desire to change lanes. This notifies other drivers of your planned move.
   - Check Your Blind Spots: Turn your head and check your blind spots over your shoulder to verify there are no cars or obstructions in the next lane.

➢ Plan Your Move: Select a sufficient gap in traffic that enables you to merge smoothly into the target lane.

➢ Gradual Steering: Begin to steer towards the neighboring lane while maintaining a steady and controlled movement. Avoid abrupt or rapid lane changes.

➢ Maintain pace: Match your pace to the flow of traffic in the new lane to ensure a seamless changeover and avoid interrupting the traffic pattern.

➢ Cancel Your Turn Signal: Once you have completed the lane change, remember to turn off your turn signal to prevent misleading other drivers.

2. Making Turns:

➢ Signal Your Intentions: Activate your turn signal in advance to alert other vehicles of your intention to make a turn. Signal for at least 100 feet (30 meters) before the turn on conventional roads, and signal at least five seconds before the turn on highways.

➢ Position Your car: Position your car in the suitable lane for the intended turn. Use lane markers and road signs as guidance.

➢ Cede to Pedestrians: If there are pedestrians crossing the road, always cede the right-of-way to them. Be attentive and check for pedestrians in crosswalks and at crossings.

➢ Slow Down: Reduce your speed before making the turn, particularly for abrupt or tight curves. This helps maintain control and stability.

➢ Check for Oncoming Traffic: Look for oncoming traffic and determine that it is safe to continue with the turn. Observe the flow of traffic from all directions, including automobiles, bikes, and pedestrians.

➢ Maintain the Proper Turning route: Follow the proper turning route for the sort of turn you are performing. Stay inside your lane and avoid cutting corners or straying into adjacent lanes.

➢ Complete the Turn: Steer smoothly and steadily through the turn, keeping a steady speed. Accelerate slightly as you leave the corner to meet the flow of traffic.

Always remember to stay alert of your surroundings, utilize your mirrors efficiently, and check blind spots while changing lanes or making turns. Observe traffic regulations, signals, and road markers to guarantee safe and legal movements. By practicing these strategies and being aware of other road users, you may negotiate lane changes and turns with confidence and create a safer driving environment for everyone.

Handling junctions and roundabouts

Handling crossroads and roundabouts demands careful attention and respect to traffic laws to guarantee safe and efficient traffic movement. Here are some suggestions for negotiating junctions and roundabouts:

1. Intersections:
➢ Approach with care: Reduce your speed and approach junctions with care, searching for any possible hazards or incoming vehicles.
➢ Observe Traffic Signs and lights: Pay attention to traffic lights, stop signs, yield signs, and any other signage that prescribes the right-of-way or specified activities at the junction.
➢ Check for Pedestrians and bicycles: Look for pedestrians and bicycles crossing the junction, and surrender the right-of-way to them when appropriate.

2. Left Turns:
➢ When performing a left turn, place your vehicle in the proper lane and yield to incoming traffic.
➢ Wait for a safe space in incoming traffic before making the turn.
➢ Use your turn signal to express your desire to turn left.

3. Right Turns:

➢ When performing a right turn, approach the junction in the rightmost lane, unless lane markings indicate otherwise.

➢ Yield to pedestrians, bicycles, and oncoming traffic (where appropriate).

➢ Use your turn signal to express your desire to turn right.

4. Straight Through:

➢ When continuing straight through an intersection, maintain your lane position and yield to any cars already at the junction.

➢ Use your turn signal to express your desire to travel straight.

5. Roundabouts:

➢ Approach and Yield: Slow down and yield to cars already in the circle. Observe yield signs if present.

➢ Choose the Correct Lane: Use the proper lane for your desired departure. Follow lane markers and signs.

➢ Reduce Speed: Adjust your speed according to the flow of traffic inside the roundabout. Maintain a safe distance from the car ahead.

➢ Yield to Pedestrians and bicycles: Give the right-of-way to pedestrians and bicycles at crosswalks or approaching the roundabout.

6. Enter the Roundabout:

- ➢ When there is a safe break in traffic, enter the roundabout by turning right and merging smoothly.
- ➢ Use your turn signal to announce your desire to enter the roundabout.
- ➢ Maintain Lane Position: Stay inside your lane and do not change lanes within the roundabout.
7. Exit the Roundabout:
- ➢ Signal your desire to depart the roundabout in advance.
- ➢ Watch for pedestrians and bikers as you approach your exit.
- ➢ Exit the roundabout smoothly and yield to any cars remaining inside the circle.

Always be attention, respect traffic regulations, and be mindful of other road users while traversing crossroads and roundabouts. Yield the right-of-way when needed, utilize your turn signals efficiently, and maintain a safe speed and distance from other cars. By adopting these tactics, you can safely and effectively manage various traffic scenarios.

Parking and backing moves

Parking and backing procedures are vital skills to acquire for safe and efficient vehicle operation. Whether you're parallel parking, perpendicular parking, or doing other backup maneuvers, it's vital to follow precise practices. Here are some recommendations for parking and backing:

1. Parallel Parking:

➤ Choose a Suitable Parking Space:

➤ Look for a location that is big enough to fit your car, leaving adequate area to move.

➤ Check for any parking restrictions or laws in the area.

2. Position Your Vehicle:

➤ Pull up parallel to the car in front of the parking place, allowing approximately two to three feet of space between the vehicles.

➤ Align the back bumpers of both autos.

3. Backing into the Space:

➤ Check for traffic, pedestrians, and bicycles before making the move.

➤ Begin reversing gently while rotating your driving wheel completely to the right.

➤ Continuously watch your surrounds, utilizing your mirrors and peering over your shoulder to assure clearance.

➤ Straighten your steering wheel as your car aligns with the vehicle behind.

➤ Once parked, adjust your position if required and confirm your car is inside the assigned parking area.

- Apply the parking brake and shift to Park (P) or select the appropriate gear for your car.
- Perpendicular Parking (90-Degree Parking):

4. Select an Appropriate Space:
- Look for a location that is broad enough to fit your car comfortably.
- Be careful of any parking restrictions or laws in the neighborhood.

5. Position Your Vehicle:
- Drive gently and place your vehicle parallel to the nearby parked automobiles.
- Align your car to enable ample room for entering and departing.

6. Backing into the Space:
- Check for traffic, pedestrians, and bicycles before commencing the move.
- Begin reversing carefully, moving your driving wheel completely to the right.
- Continuously check your mirrors and peek over your shoulder for clearance.
- Straighten your steering wheel as your car lines with the parking place.
- Adjust your location as required and verify your car is inside the approved parking lines.

➢ Apply the parking brake and shift to Park (P) or select the appropriate gear for your car.

7. Assess the Area:

➢ Before backing up, scan the surroundings for any impediments, pedestrians, or incoming cars.

➢ Use your mirrors and swivel your head to check blind areas.

8. Activate Your Hazard Lights:

➢ Turn on your hazard lights to signify that you are executing a backup motion.

9. Back Up Slowly:

➢ Engage reverse gear and begin backing up carefully while retaining complete control of the vehicle.

➢ Continuously examine your mirrors and surroundings for any changes.

10. Steer and Look Backward:

➢ Steer gently and gradually, keeping a constant check on the back of your vehicle.

➢ Look straight out the back window or utilize rearview cameras if available.

11. Make Small Adjustments:

➢ If required, make tiny modifications to your steering or speed to ensure safe and controlled backing.

12. Proceed with Caution:

➢ Back up only as far as required, given the stated aim of the move.

➢ When done, change to Drive (D) or the appropriate gear for your car.

Remember to practice these parking and backing procedures in a safe and controlled setting before trying them in real-world scenarios. Be patient, mindful of your surroundings, and maintain excellent sight during the move. By following these recommendations, you may securely park and conduct backing maneuvers with confidence.

CHAPTER 5: Driver Responsibility and Licensing

Licensing requirements and procedures

Driver Responsibility and Licensing are crucial parts of ensuring safe and responsible driving. Understanding the licensing standards and processes is vital for acquiring and keeping a valid driver's license. Here are some major considerations about licensing requirements and procedures:

1. Licensing Requirements:

➢ Minimum Age: The minimum age required for acquiring a driver's license differs based on the jurisdiction. Generally, it is between 16 and 18 years old. Check with your local Department of Motor Vehicles (DMV) for the precise age restrictions in your region.

➢ Identification papers: You will normally need to present identification papers, such as a birth certificate, passport, or social security card, to confirm your identity.

➢ Knowledge exam: You will be needed to complete a written knowledge exam that tests your awareness of traffic rules, road signs, and safe driving practices. The DMV offers study resources to assist you prepare for the exam.

➤ Vision Test: A vision test is undertaken to check that you have appropriate eyesight to drive safely. If required, you may need to wear corrective glasses while driving.

➤ Driver Education: Some states or jurisdictions mandate completion of a driver education course or program before acquiring a driver's license, particularly for adolescent drivers.

➤ Behind-the-Wheel instruction: In addition to the written exam, you may need to complete a specific number of hours of behind-the-wheel instruction with a trained instructor or a licensed adult.

➤ Driving Skills exam: After satisfying the relevant prerequisites, you will need to pass a driving skills exam that measures your ability to drive a car safely on the road. The exam often entails displaying different movements, respecting traffic regulations, and exhibiting defensive driving tactics.

2. Licensing Procedures:

➤ Application Process: Visit your local DMV office to present the appropriate papers, complete the application form, and pay the necessary costs.

➤ Written exam: Schedule an appointment to take the written knowledge exam. Study the driver's handbook or any other study materials given by the DMV to prepare for the exam.

➢ Vision Test: Your eyesight will be checked to confirm that you fulfill the minimal visual acuity criteria.

➢ Behind-the-Wheel instruction: If necessary, complete the requisite hours of behind-the-wheel instruction with a competent teacher or a licensed adult.

➢ Driving Skills exam: Once you have completed all the qualifications, arrange an appointment for the driving skills exam. Bring a vehicle that fulfills the DMV's standards for the test.

➢ License Issuance: If you pass the driving abilities exam, you will be awarded a driver's license. The sort of license you acquire may depend on your age, the type of vehicle you are authorized to drive, and any limitations or endorsements relevant to your license.

It's crucial to remember that licensing requirements and processes may differ based on your jurisdiction. Therefore, it is essential to visit your local DMV or licensing office for particular information pertinent to your location.

Remember, driving is a privilege that comes with responsibility. Adhering to traffic regulations, adopting safe driving behaviors, and regularly upgrading your knowledge and abilities are vital for retaining a valid driver's license and protecting the safety of yourself and others on the road.

Driver's license courses and endorsements

Driver's license classes and endorsements are further classifications that identify the sorts of cars you are permitted to drive and any other driving privileges you may have. Here are some frequent driver's license courses and endorsements:

1. Driver's License Classes:

➢ Class A: This class often enables the operation of combination vehicles, such as tractor-trailers or truck and trailer combinations, with a gross vehicle weight rating (GVWR) surpassing a particular threshold. Class A license holders may also drive cars in lower classes.

➢ Class B: This class normally enables the operation of single vehicles with a GVWR surpassing a particular threshold, such as huge buses, dump trucks, or delivery trucks. Class B license holders may also drive cars in lower classes.

➢ Class C: This class authorizes the operation of vehicles that do not fit into Class A or Class B categories. It comprises vehicles meant to transport 16 or more people (including the driver) and vehicles carrying hazardous items needing placards.

2. Endorsements:

➢ Passenger (P) Endorsement: This endorsement permits the bearer to drive vehicles intended to carry passengers, such as buses or vans. The particular rules and constraints may differ based on the jurisdiction.

➢ School Bus (S) Endorsement: This endorsement enables the operating of school buses. It often involves extra training and certification relevant to the operation of school buses and the transporting of kids.

➢ Hazardous Materials (H) Endorsement: This endorsement is mandatory for drivers who carry hazardous materials. It entails completing a written exam and conducting a security threat assessment.

➢ Motorcycle (M) Endorsement: This endorsement is necessary for operating motorbikes. It may require completing a written exam and a practical skills test particularly intended for motorbikes.

➢ Tank Vehicle (N) Endorsement: This endorsement authorizes the operation of vehicles that carry liquids or gases in bulk containers, such as tank trucks. Additional knowledge and abilities unique to managing tank vehicles may be necessary.

It's crucial to remember that the availability of licensing classes and endorsements, as well as the particular criteria and processes, may differ depending on your jurisdiction. Therefore, it is essential to visit your local Department of Motor Vehicles (DMV) or licensing body for specific information about license classes and endorsements relevant in your region.

Obtaining extra licensing classes and endorsements often includes completing certain criteria, such as passing knowledge examinations, practical skills tests, or receiving further training. Always verify that you carry the right license class and endorsements for the cars you want to drive to comply with legal requirements and guarantee safe driving practices.

Vehicle registration and insurance

Vehicle registration and insurance are key legal and financial duties for vehicle owners. Here's an overview of automobile registration and insurance:

1. Vehicle Registration:
➢ Initial Registration: When you acquire a car, you must register it with the relevant government agency, often the

Department of Motor Vehicles (DMV) or a comparable body in your area.

➢ Required Documentation: To register your car, you will normally need to present the following documents:

➢ Proof of ownership, such as a title or bill of sale

➢ Proof of identity, such as your driver's license or identification card

➢ Proof of residence, which may include utility bills or lease agreements

➢ A completed registration application form, issued by the DMV

➢ Payment for the registration costs and any relevant taxes

➢ Vehicle Inspection: Some jurisdictions need a safety inspection or emissions test to guarantee that your vehicle meets particular criteria. Check with your local DMV to learn whether an inspection is necessary in your region.

➢ License Plates and Registration Stickers: Once you have finished the registration procedure and paid the costs, you will be granted license plates and registration stickers that must be applied to your vehicle as evidence of proper registration.

Renewal: Vehicle registrations often expire after a specified term, usually one year. It is your obligation to renew your registration before it expires to avoid penalties or fines.

2. Vehicle Insurance:

Legal Requirement: In most areas, obtaining proper automobile insurance is obligatory. It offers financial protection in case of accidents, property damage, or injuries caused by your car.

➤ Kinds of Coverage: Vehicle insurance plans often contain the following kinds of coverage:

➤ Liability Coverage: This covers damages and injuries you may cause to others in an accident.

➤ Accident Coverage: This covers damages to your own car in event of an accident, regardless of responsibility.

➤ Comprehensive Coverage: This covers damages to your car arising from non-collision situations, such as theft, vandalism, or natural catastrophes.

➤ Personal harm Protection (PIP) or Medical Payments Coverage: This covers medical expenditures for you and your passengers in case of harm.

➤ Uninsured/Underinsured Motorist Coverage: This covers damages and injuries caused by uninsured or underinsured drivers.

➤ Insurance Provider: Choose an insurance provider and coverage that meets your requirements. Shop around, compare estimates, and consider aspects like as coverage limitations, deductibles, and customer service reputation.

➢ Proof of Insurance: You will normally need to carry proof of insurance in your vehicle at all times. Insurance firms give insurance cards or policy papers that act as evidence of coverage.

➢ Renewal: Insurance plans normally have a period of six months or one year. It is crucial to renew your insurance policy before it expires to preserve ongoing coverage.

It's crucial to follow the registration and insurance requirements unique to your area. Failure to register your car or maintain current insurance coverage may result in fines, penalties, and legal implications. Consult your local DMV or insurance provider for additional information about car registration and insurance requirements in your region.

Responsibilities and punishments for traffic infractions

Responsibilities and punishments for traffic offenses differ based on the jurisdiction and the individual infringement committed. However, here are some typical obligations and punishments linked with traffic violations:

1. Responsibilities:

- Adherence to Traffic rules: It is the obligation of every motorist to respect traffic rules and regulations. This involves respecting speed limits, traffic lights, and road signs, as well as surrendering right-of-way where necessary.

- Safe Driving Practices: Drivers are required to adopt safe driving tactics, such as keeping a reasonable following distance, utilizing turn signals, and avoiding hazardous behaviors like speeding or distracted driving.

- Vehicle Maintenance: Keeping your vehicle in perfect operational condition is vital for road safety. Regular maintenance, including functional brakes, lights, and tires, is vital.

2. Penalties:

- penalties: Traffic offenses frequently result in monetary penalties. The amount of the fine depends on the severity of the infraction and may vary based on the jurisdiction.

- License Points: Many jurisdictions have a point system where points are issued to a driver's record for each infraction. Accumulating too many points within a certain span may lead to license suspension or other repercussions.

- License Suspension or Revocation: Serious or repetitive violations may result in the suspension or revocation of your driver's license. The duration of the suspension or revocation depends on the severity of the offence and your driving history.

➢ Traffic School: In certain situations, drivers may be obliged to attend traffic school as part of the punishment for a traffic infringement. This may assist decrease the effect on your driving record or complete criteria to restore a suspended license.

➢ Increased Insurance Rates: Traffic offenses may lead to an increase in insurance prices. Insurance companies may see infractions as a sign of increased risk, resulting in higher premiums or policy termination.

➢ Criminal prosecution: Certain traffic infractions, such as driving under the influence (DUI), reckless driving, or hit-and-run occurrences, may lead to criminal prosecution. The penalty for these infractions may include fines, license suspension, probation, community service, or even incarceration.

➢ It's crucial to understand that traffic violation fines may vary greatly based on the jurisdiction and the precise circumstances of the infraction. It is essential to check your local Department of Motor Vehicles (DMV) or legal counsel for complete information on the duties and fines connected with traffic offenses in your region.

Remember, practicing safe and responsible driving is vital for your personal safety, the safety of others on the road, and to avoid the legal and financial penalties of traffic offences.

Implications of distracted driving and cell phone usage

Distracted driving, especially due to mobile phone usage, may have significant repercussions for road safety. Here are the primary consequences of distracted driving and mobile phone use:

➢ Increased Risk of Accidents: Engaging in distracted driving, such as texting, chatting on the phone, or using mobile applications, diverts your attention from the road and diminishes your ability to respond to possible risks. This dramatically increases the danger of accidents, including collisions with other cars, pedestrians, or immovable objects.

➢ Hampered Reaction Time: When your concentration is focused on a mobile phone or other distractions, your ability to respond swiftly to changing road conditions or unexpected occurrences is hampered. This delayed response time might have disastrous effects, since split-second judgments and moves may be vital for averting accidents.

➤ Reduced Situational Awareness: Using a mobile phone while driving might impair your situational awareness. Your attention gets absorbed on the phone screen or the discussion, allowing you to overlook critical visual cues, traffic signs, and signals. This lack of awareness may lead to lane exits, failure to yield, or other traffic offenses.

➤ Poor Control and unpredictable Driving: Distracted driving generally leads in poor vehicle control and unpredictable driving behavior. Engaging in things like texting involves physical dexterity, which may lead to swerving, drifting between lanes, or unexpected stopping. Such movements might startle other drivers and increase the danger of accidents.

➤ Increased Likelihood of Injuries and deaths: Distracted driving-related incidents are known to cause major injuries and deaths. The combination of shortened response time, impaired situational awareness, and unpredictable driving behavior considerably heightens the risks of catastrophic consequences in the case of an accident.

➤ Legal Consequences: Many jurisdictions have adopted rules and regulations that particularly target mobile phone usage while driving. Violating these rules may result in fines, license points, license suspension, or even criminal charges, depending on the severity of the infraction and local restrictions.

➢ Higher Insurance prices: Distracted driving occurrences might lead to an increase in insurance prices. Insurance companies see inattentive driving as a dangerous practice, which may result in increased rates or even policy cancellation.

➢ To increase road safety and limit the consequences of distracted driving, it is vital to prevent mobile phone usage while operating a vehicle. Instead, adopt appropriate driving practices such as keeping your phone out of reach, utilizing hands-free devices for important calls, and pulling over to a safe spot if you need to use your phone or indulge in any other distracting activity.

Remember, your whole attention and concentration should be on the road when driving. By minimizing distractions and emphasizing safety, you contribute to a safer driving environment for yourself and others on the road.

Understanding the point system and license suspensions

The point system and license suspensions are measures used by licensing authorities to encourage safe driving behaviors and hold drivers responsible for traffic offenses. Here's an outline of the point system and license suspension process:

1. Point System:

➢ Accumulating Points: Under the point system, each traffic infringement is allocated a certain amount of points. When a motorist commits a violation, points are added to their driving record.

➢ Point Values: The point values allocated to offenses vary based on the jurisdiction and the severity of the crime. More significant breaches often have greater point values.

➢ Thresholds: The point system normally has a threshold or limit within a defined period. If a motorist collects points over this level, they may face penalties such as license suspension or other punishments.

➢ Point term: Points on a driving record normally have a term during which they stay active. After a set time, points may be erased from the driving record, decreasing the overall point count.

2. License Suspension:

➢ Reaching the Suspension level: When a motorist collects points over the prescribed level during a defined term, their license may be subject to suspension. The criterion and term for license suspension varies by jurisdiction.

➢ Notification: The licensing authority will normally inform the motorist of the imminent license suspension. This communication may contain information regarding the period of the suspension and any criteria for restoring the license.

➢ Suspension Period: The period of the license suspension depends on the jurisdiction and the amount of collected points. Typically, the suspension term rises with the amount of points and the frequency of offenses.

➢ Reinstatement conditions: To restore a suspended license, the driver normally has to meet specific conditions, which may include serving the suspension time, paying reinstatement costs, completing any necessary educational programs or defensive driving courses, or passing extra examinations.

➢ Repeat Offenses: Repeat infractions or subsequent license suspensions within a specific timeframe may lead to longer suspension durations, harsher fines, or possibly permanent revocation of the driver's license.

It's crucial to understand that the point system and license suspension procedure might differ across jurisdictions. The particular point values allocated to offenses, the length of points on a driving record, and the suspension criteria may change. Therefore, it is essential to visit your local Department of Motor Vehicles (DMV) or licensing authority for complete information on the point system and license suspension processes relevant in your region.

By knowing the point system and the possible repercussions of accruing points, drivers may make educated judgments, adopt safe driving practices, and take appropriate efforts to keep a clean driving record.

CHAPTER 6: Special Driving Situations

Driving in unfavorable weather circumstances (rain, fog, snow, etc.)

Driving in poor weather conditions takes additional vigilance and adaptations to guarantee safety on the road. Here are some suggestions for driving in typical severe weather conditions:

1. Rain:
➢ Slow down: Reduce your speed and maintain a safe following distance from the car ahead.
➢ Use windshield wipers and headlights: Turn on your headlights and use your windshield wipers to increase visibility.
➢ Avoid rapid maneuvers: Steer and stop carefully to avoid skidding or hydroplaning on wet roads.
➢ Be careful of other drivers: Watch out for other cars, particularly bigger ones that may cause spray and impair visibility.
2. Fog:
➢ Slow down and use low beams: Reduce your speed slightly and use low beams or fog lights to boost visibility.

➢ Avoid high lights: High beams might bounce off the fog, further lowering vision. Use them exclusively in extremely low traffic regions.

➢ Use windshield defogger and wipers: Keep your windshield clear to retain visibility.

➢ Listen for traffic: Roll down your windows slightly to listen for oncoming cars.

3. Snow and Ice:

➢ Drive slowly: Reduce your speed and drive at a rate suited for the road circumstances.

➢ Increase following distance: Leave adequate space between your car and the one ahead to allow for longer stopping distances.

➢ Use winter tires or chains: If required, equip your vehicle with winter tires or use chains to increase traction.

➢ Be careful on bridges and overpasses: These structures ice quicker than conventional roadways, so take particular caution while crossing them.

4. Strong Winds:

➢ Keep a tight hold on the steering wheel: Strong gusts might impact your vehicle's steadiness. Maintain a tight grasp to remain in control.

➢ Be wary of other vehicles: Large vehicles like trucks or trailers might be more influenced by severe winds. Give them more room and be careful while passing.

➢ Reduce speed: Decrease your speed to adjust for the influence of crosswinds.

➢ Watch out for debris: Strong winds might create debris or fallen branches on the road. Stay careful and avoid any impediments.

Remember, if weather conditions get too severe or if you feel dangerous, consider finding a safe spot to pull over and wait for the weather to improve. Your safety and the safety of others should always be your primary concern while driving in poor weather conditions.

Nighttime driving and usage of headlights

Nighttime driving demands extra attention and the right usage of headlights to maintain safety on the road. Here are some guidelines for nighttime driving and the usage of headlights:

1. Use headlights:

➢ Turn on your headlights: As daylight fades, turn on your headlights to maximize your visibility to other vehicles and pedestrians.

➢ Use low beams: Unless essential, use low beams instead than high lights to prevent blinding approaching traffic.

➢ High beam usage: When there are no incoming cars or vehicles ahead, you may activate high beams to boost visibility. However, swiftly switch to low lights when approaching or following another vehicle.

2. Maintain headlamp condition:

➢ Clean headlights: Regularly clean your headlights to eliminate dirt, dust, and debris that might impair their efficacy.

➢ Aim headlights properly: Ensure that your headlights are suitably pointed to give best lighting of the road without blinding other drivers.

3. Increase visibility:

➢ Keep windshield and mirrors clean: A clean windshield and correctly adjusted mirrors assist improve your field of view.

➢ Use interior lights sparingly: Bright interior lights might hamper your ability to see outdoors, so use them sparingly.

4. Be aware and cautious:

➢ Reduce speed: Decrease your speed while nighttime driving to allow for longer response times and higher stopping distances.

➤ Watch for pedestrians: Pedestrians may be difficult to spot at night, so be careful at crosswalks and in areas with foot activity.

➤ Stay focused: Avoid distractions and keep attention to the road and your surroundings.

5. Take breaks if needed:

➤ If you feel exhausted or sleepy, take frequent pauses to relax and replenish yourself. Fatigue may greatly affect your driving ability, particularly at night.

Remember, nighttime driving brings extra obstacles owing to limited visibility. By utilizing headlights appropriately, keeping attention, and adopting defensive driving tactics, you may help assure your safety and the safety of others on the road.

Driving in work zones and construction locations

Driving in work zones and construction regions demands particular care and attention to guarantee the safety of both drivers and construction employees. Here are some crucial suggestions for managing work zones and construction areas:

➤ Reduce speed: Slow down and adhere to the imposed speed restrictions in work zones. Reduced speeds are essential to accommodate for changing road conditions and the presence of construction personnel and equipment.

➢ Follow signage and instructions: Pay special attention to signs, cones, and flaggers guiding traffic. Follow their directions and merge as recommended to preserve a smooth flow of traffic.

➢ Maintain a safe following distance: Increase your following distance to accommodate for abrupt stops or slower traffic in work zones. This gives you with adequate time to respond to any unforeseen occurrences.

➢ Watch for employees and equipment: Be aware for construction workers, their cars, and equipment approaching or departing the work zone. Keep an eye for flaggers indicating traffic and be prepared to yield when required.

➢ Avoid distractions: Minimize distractions within your car. Avoid using your phone, eating, or indulging in any activity that diverts your attention from the road. Focusing completely on driving boosts your awareness and response time.

➢ Merge smoothly: When merging into a single lane or when lanes are altered, be polite and let cars to merge one at a time. Use your turn signals to express your intentions and create seamless lane changes.

➢ Be patient and calm: Traffic delays are usual in work zones, so exercise patience and be cool. Aggressive driving actions may cause dangers and increase the chance of accidents.

➢ Observe work zone speed cameras: Some work zones may be equipped with speed cameras to monitor and enforce speed restrictions. Adhere to the specified limits to avoid obtaining traffic penalties.

➢ Plan ahead and allow additional time: Before your travel, check for any scheduled work zones along your route. Plan your itinerary appropriately, giving you additional time to go through these locations.

➢ Respect the employees' safety: Remember that construction workers are doing their duties to enhance road conditions. Show them respect by driving gently and responsibly.

By following these principles, you may help protect the safety of both yourself and anyone working in construction zones. Always practice patience, keep aware, and adjust to changing situations to traverse work zones efficiently.

Sharing the road with huge vehicles (trucks, buses)

Sharing the road with huge vehicles such as trucks and buses demands additional care and a grasp of their peculiarities. Here are some crucial recommendations for safely sharing the road with these vehicles:

➤ Maintain a safe distance: Large cars take more time and space to stop, so maintain a safe following distance. Avoid tailgating and leave them adequate room to move.

➤ Avoid blind areas: Large cars have substantial blind spots, notably on the right side, rear, and immediately behind them. Stay clear of these blind zones by either slowing down or speeding up to pass safely.

➤ Use your mirrors and signals: Before changing lanes or making changes near big cars, check your mirrors attentively, and use your turn signals to express your intentions early. This helps the drivers of heavy vehicles anticipate your activities.

➤ Be patient while passing: while passing a huge vehicle, ensure you have adequate open space ahead. Signal your purpose, speed gently, and pass them on the left side. Avoid cutting in front too closely, since heavy trucks require more time to stop.

➤ Give them room to make wide turns: Large trucks require a broader turning radius. If you detect a truck or bus indicating to make a right turn, leave them adequate room and avoid attempting to squeeze by on their right side.

➤ Be careful at junctions: Large vehicles may have restricted sight at intersections, so proceed with caution. Ensure that the driver recognizes your presence before making any movements.

➤ Stay visible: Make yourself visible to big vehicle drivers by keeping your headlights on, particularly during severe weather or low-light circumstances. This helps people recognize your presence on the road.

➤ Anticipate their actions: Large cars have distinct acceleration and deceleration rates compared to smaller ones. Anticipate their movements and adapt your driving appropriately to keep a safe distance.

➤ Be careful of crosswinds: Crosswinds may impact the stability of heavy vehicles. If you are driving near or passing a huge truck under windy conditions, be prepared for abrupt moves and keep a steady route.

➤ Report risky driving conduct: If you witness a huge vehicle driving recklessly or showing dangerous behavior, report it to the proper authorities. Your actions may help avert possible mishaps.

Remember, exercising patience, keeping distance, and being aware of the limits of huge vehicles are crucial to sharing the road safely. By following these recommendations, you contribute to a safer driving environment for everyone on the road.

Navigating across roads and freeways

Navigating through roads and freeways effectively and safely needs appropriate planning, attentiveness, and attention to traffic laws. Here are some crucial suggestions to assist you negotiate these high-speed roadways:

➢ Plan your route: Before joining the highway or motorway, acquaint yourself with the route and any exits or interchanges you need to take. Use GPS navigation or maps to keep informed of approaching turns and lane changes.

➢ Merge safely: When entering a highway or motorway, match your speed to the flow of traffic and utilize the on-ramp to merge smoothly. Signal your intentions early, check your blind zones, and yield to cars already on the route.

➢ select the proper lane: Observe the displayed signs and select the appropriate lane for your destination. Typically, the right lane is for slower-moving traffic, while the left lanes are for passing at faster speeds. Follow the flow of traffic and avoid continuously changing lanes.

➢ Maintain a safe following distance: Keep a safe distance from the vehicle ahead to allow for ample stopping space. The conventional norm is to maintain at least a 3-second space, rising to 4 or more seconds under severe weather or heavy traffic circumstances.

➢ Use turn signals: Signal your intentions early and use your turn signals while changing lanes, merging, or leaving the highway. This helps other drivers anticipate your behavior and facilitates better traffic flow.

➢ Observe speed restrictions: Adhere to the established speed limits on highways and freeways. Keep in mind that these limitations are intended for best safety and traffic flow. Adjust your speed to meet the current circumstances, such as heavy traffic or poor weather.

➢ Stay attentive and avoid distractions: Highways and highways need your whole concentration. Avoid distractions like as texting, chatting on the phone, or indulging in other activities that draw your concentration away from the road.

➢ Be alert of exits and interchanges: Pay attention to signage signaling future exits and interchanges. Plan your lane changes and merging well in advance to ensure you take the proper exit or continue on the intended path.

➢ Stay in your lane: Avoid excessive lane changes and weaving between lanes. Maintain a steady pace and employ lane changes only when required, such as when leaving or overtaking slower cars.

➢ Be prepared for high-speed driving: Be careful of the greater speeds on roads and freeways. Adjust your driving appropriately, be vigilant, and be aware of the activities of other drivers.

Remember, cautious driving tactics and respect to traffic laws are vital while traversing motorways and freeways. Stay vigilant, anticipate possible risks, and keep a safe and steady speed to guarantee a smooth and safe voyage.

Transporting persons and goods safely

Transporting individuals and freight securely needs careful attention to different elements to safeguard their well-being and the security of the objects being carried. Here are some basic guidelines for safe transportation:

➢ car Inspection: Before each journey, examine your car completely to verify it is in perfect operational condition.

Check the tires, brakes, lights, and other key components to prevent any mechanical troubles throughout the ride.

➢ Secure goods: Properly secure and distribute the goods to avoid moving or dropping during travel. Use proper restraints, such as straps or cargo netting, to hold the things in place. Distribute the weight equally to ensure vehicle balance.

➢ Passenger Safety: If you are carrying passengers, check sure they are wearing seat belts and that the vehicle has enough seating capacity. Educate passengers on the necessity of seat belt use and enforce laws for their safety.

➢ Defensive Driving: Practice defensive driving tactics to anticipate and react to possible risks. Maintain a safe following distance, remain aware of your surroundings, and avoid aggressive movements that might jeopardize your passengers or cargo.

➢ Adhere to Speed restrictions: Observe and respect the imposed speed restrictions. Driving at an acceptable pace enables greater control of the vehicle and decreases the danger of accidents. Adjust your speed dependent on road and weather conditions.

➢ Avoid Distractions: Minimize distractions within the car to keep attention on the road. Avoid using mobile phones, eating, or indulging in activities that draw your focus away from driving.

➢ Regular Maintenance: Schedule regular car maintenance to maintain it in optimum condition. Regularly inspect and maintain the engine, brakes, suspension, and other important components to avoid failures or malfunctions.

➢ prepare Rest breaks: If the travel is lengthy, prepare for frequent rest breaks to avoid driving weariness. Fatigue may decrease judgment and response times, so take pauses and rest when required to guarantee alertness during the journey.

➢ Weather Considerations: Adjust your driving style and pace according to weather conditions. Exercise care while driving in inclement weather, such as rain, snow, or fog, since it may influence road traction and visibility.

➢ Follow Traffic Rules: Observe all traffic rules, signals, and regulations to guarantee the safety of your passengers, goods, and other road users. Respect traffic signs, signals, and right-of-way restrictions.

Remember, the safety of passengers and the integrity of the goods are crucial. By following these suggestions and adopting safe driving habits, you may guarantee a secure and enjoyable travel for everyone involved.

CHAPTER 7: Road Signs, Signals, and Markings

Understanding and understanding traffic signs and symbols

Understanding and understanding traffic signs, signals, and markings is vital for safe and responsible driving. Here are the primary sorts of traffic signs, signals, and markings you should be acquainted with:

1. Regulatory Signs:

These signs identify and enforce traffic rules and regulations. Examples include stop signs, yield signs, speed restriction signs, and no-entry signs. It's crucial to respect these signs to guarantee the safety of all road users.

2. Warning Signs:

These signs inform drivers of possible risks ahead. They may signal bends, steep hills, pedestrian crossings, animal crossings, and other possible risks. Pay careful attention to these indicators and change your driving appropriately.

3. Guide Signs:

These signs give information about routes, destinations, services, and amenities. They assist drivers navigate and organize their routes. Examples include highway route signs, exit signs, and signage denoting rest places, petrol stations, and tourist sites.

4. Informational Signs:

These signs give more information or direction to drivers. They may contain signs showing distances, parking laws, construction zones, and road conditions ahead. Pay attention to these signs to be updated about any changes or exceptional circumstances.

5. Traffic Signals:

Traffic signals govern the flow of traffic at crossings. They contain red, yellow, and green lights that signal when to halt, slow down, or progress. Obey traffic lights and observe the right-of-way laws linked with them.

6. Pavement Markings:

These markings on the road surface give direction and information to drivers. They include lane lines, crosswalks, stop lines, and arrows indicating direction. Follow these markers to ensure appropriate lane location and manage junctions properly.

7. Symbols and International Signs:

Some road signs employ symbols or are standardized worldwide to communicate information across language boundaries. Examples include emblems denoting hospitals, airports, and cycling lanes. Familiarize yourself with these symbols to comprehend their significance.

It's crucial to learn and comprehend these road signs, signals, and markings before taking your driving test and for safe driving in general. Make sure to frequently examine them and remain current on any changes or additions in your local region. Remember, road signs and markings serve a critical role in directing and regulating traffic, guaranteeing the safety and efficiency of road users.

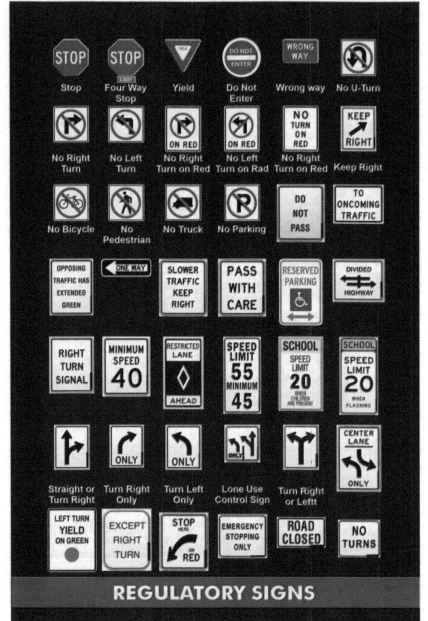

REGULATORY SIGNS

PAVEMENT MARKING

Solid Yellow and Broken
Yellow Centerline

Double Solid Yellow Line

Single Broken Yellow Line

Center Turning Lane

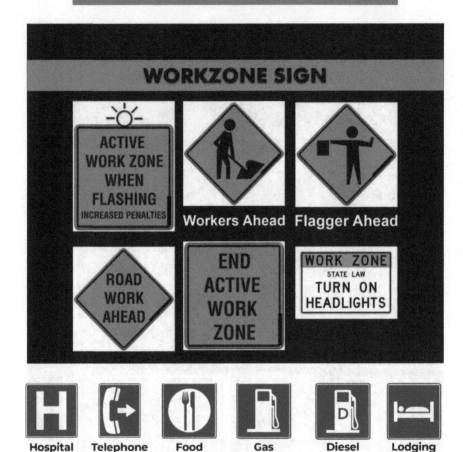

Traffic signals and their meanings

Traffic signals are a vital feature of the traffic management system, controlling the flow of cars and pedestrians at crossings. Here are the typical traffic lights and their meanings:

1. Red Light:

A red light signifies halt. You must come to a full stop before the appropriate stop line or crosswalk. Remain halted until the light turns to green.

2. Green Light:

A green light implies go. When the light turns green, you may go across the crossing, but always yield to pedestrians and vehicles already at the intersection or arriving from other directions.

3. Yellow Light:

A yellow light signals that the light is ready to shift to red. It acts as a warning to prepare to quit. If you can safely stop before reaching the junction, do so. Otherwise, go gently through the crossing, but do not speed to beat the red light.

4. Green Arrow:

A green arrow signal lets you to make a protected turn in the direction of the arrow. Yield to any pedestrians or cars remaining in the intersection and complete your turn safely. Remember to observe the right-of-way regulations particular to the arrow.

5. Flashing Red Light:

A flashing red light is handled the same as a stop sign. Come to a full stop, yield to other cars or pedestrians, and continue when it is safe to do so.

6. Flashing Yellow Light:

A flashing yellow light denotes caution. Slow down and go through the junction with care, yielding to any pedestrians or cars in the intersection.

7. Pedestrian Signals:

Pedestrian signals are often situated near crosswalks. The "Walk" signal permits pedestrians to cross the street, whereas the "Don't Walk" or flashing hand signal advises that pedestrians should not start crossing or should stop crossing if already in the roadway.

It's crucial to pay attention to traffic lights, obey their directions, and be careful of other road users while approaching junctions. Understanding and following traffic signals encourages safe and orderly traffic flow, lowering the likelihood of accidents and guaranteeing the safety of all road users.

Pavement markings and their relevance

Pavement markings serve a critical role in giving direction, information, and restrictions to drivers on the road. Here are some popular pavement marks and their significance:

1. Lane Markings:

Lane markings are solid or dashed lines that denote the division between lanes of traffic. They assist drivers maintain their lane position and control traffic flow. The numerous forms of lane markers include:

➢ Solid White Line: A solid white line implies that lane changes are discouraged. Stay in your lane until required, and do not cross the line unless it is safe to do so.

➢ Dashed White Line: A dashed white line facilitates lane changes. You may cross the line when it is safe and essential, after checking for other cars.

➢ Solid Yellow Line: A solid yellow line signifies that passing is banned in most instances. Stay in your lane and do not cross the line to pass other cars.

➢ Dashed Yellow Line: A dashed yellow line indicates that passing is permitted when it is safe to do so. You may cross the line to pass another car if there are no incoming vehicles.

➢ Crosswalks: Crosswalk markers are often seen at intersections or designated pedestrian crossing locations. They show where pedestrians should cross the road. Drivers must yield to pedestrians at crosswalks and take care in these places.

➢ Stop Lines: Stop lines are solid white lines situated before junctions. They indicate where cars should come to a full stop when confronted with a stop sign or red traffic light. Vehicles should wait behind the stop line until it is safe to continue.

➢ Yield Lines: Yield lines are dashed white lines that show where cars should yield to other traffic. They are commonly spotted near yield signs or while merging into traffic. Yield to other cars or pedestrians while crossing yield lines.

➢ Arrows: Arrows painted on the road give directional instructions for cars. They show the direction of traffic in certain lanes, such as turning lanes, or assist cars through complicated junctions.

➢ Symbols and Markings: Various symbols and markings on the pavement give extra information to drivers. These include bike lane markers, parking restrictions, pedestrian symbols, and more. Familiarize yourself with these symbols and their meanings to comprehend the laws and requirements linked with them.

It's crucial to pay attention to pavement markings, since they express important information and assist ensure safe and controlled traffic flow. Observe and observe these markers to protect your personal safety and that of other road users.

Special signs and signals for train crossings, school zones, etc.

Special signs and signals serve a significant role in alerting drivers to certain scenarios and conditions on the road. Here are some examples of special signs and signals:

1. Railroad Crossing Signs:
   - ➢ Crossbuck Sign: This white sign in the form of a "X" signals a railroad crossing. It is sometimes supplemented by additional signs stating the number of tracks or whether the crossing is equipped with lights or gates.
   - ➢ Advance Warning Sign: This yellow sign with black symbols informs vehicles in advance of an oncoming railroad crossing. It acts as a warning to slow down, check for trains, and be prepared to stop if required.

➢ Flashing Lights and Gates: At certain railroad crossings, there are flashing lights and gates that activate when a train is coming. Drivers must stop and wait behind the gate until the lights stop flashing and the gate is lifted.

2. School Zone Signs:

➢ School Zone Sign: This yellow sign with black markings signifies that you are entering a school zone. Reduce your speed and be careful for minors crossing the road or strolling near the area.

➢ School Crossing Sign: This sign shows a representation of a person with a bag crossing the road. It signifies that youngsters may be crossing the road in the nearby. Exercise additional care and yield to pedestrians when you encounter this notice.

3. Construction Zone Signs:

➢ Road Work Ahead Sign: This orange sign with black symbols notifies vehicles of imminent road construction or maintenance work. Slow down, heed any detour signs, and be mindful of changing traffic patterns.

➢ Detour Signs: These signs advise cars around a construction area or blocked route. Follow the diversion signs and be prepared for temporary changes in traffic flow.

4. Pedestrian Crossing Signs:

> Pedestrian Crossing Sign: This sign contains a representation of a person walking and denotes that there is a designated pedestrian crossing. Yield to pedestrians and take care in these places.

5. Bicycle Lane Signs:

> cycling Lane Sign: This sign denotes the existence of a dedicated cycling lane. Be mindful of bicycles and avoid driving or parking in these lanes.

It's critical to pay great attention to these particular signs and signals since they give important information and instructions relevant to certain regions or situations. Adhering to these signs and signals enhances safety and helps guarantee the well-being of all road users.

CHAPTER 8: Practice Questions and Answers

Multiple-choice questions covering various topics

400 + question and answer

Goodluck on your trial!!!

1. Question: What is the purpose of a roundabout?

a) To increase traffic congestion

b) To improve traffic flow and reduce accidents

c) To create an obstacle for drivers

d) To allow pedestrians to cross easily

Answer: b) To improve traffic flow and reduce accidents

2. Question: When parking uphill with a curb, you should turn your front wheels:

a) Away from the curb

b) Toward the curb

c) Parallel to the curb

d) It doesn't matter

Answer: a) Away from the curb

3. Question: If you see a solid yellow line alongside a broken yellow line on a two-lane road, it means:

a) No passing is allowed in either direction

b) Passing is allowed only in the direction of the broken line

c) Passing is allowed only in the direction of the solid line

d) Passing is allowed in both directions

Answer: b) Passing is allowed only in the direction of the broken line

4. Question: When a traffic signal is not working at an intersection, you should:

a) Treat it as a four-way stop sign

b) Slow down and proceed with caution

c) Speed up and quickly pass through the intersection

d) Follow the direction of the vehicle in front of you

Answer: a) Treat it as a four-way stop sign

5. Question: The legal blood alcohol concentration (BAC) limit for drivers over 21 years of age in California is:

a) 0.08%

b) 0.10%

c) 0.05%

d) 0.02%

Answer: a) 0.08%

6. Question: When approaching a railroad crossing, you see flashing red lights and hear the sound of a bell. You should:

a) Stop and wait until the lights stop flashing and it is safe to proceed

b) Slow down and proceed with caution

c) Speed up and quickly cross the tracks

d) Change lanes to avoid the railroad crossing

Answer: a) Stop and wait until the lights stop flashing and it is safe to proceed

7. Question: When should you use your vehicle's horn?

a) To alert others of your presence

b) To express frustration or annoyance

c) To greet friends or family

d) To scare pedestrians or other drivers

Answer: a) To alert others of your presence

8. Question: When driving in fog, you should use your vehicle's:

a) High beam headlights

b) Low beam headlights

c) Hazard lights

d) No headlights

Answer: b) Low beam headlights

9. Question: On a freeway, the far left lane is typically used for:

a) Slower vehicles

b) Passing other vehicles

c) Trucks and commercial vehicles

d) Exiting the freeway

Answer: b) Passing other vehicles

10. Question: What does a diamond-shaped sign with an orange background indicate?

a) Construction zone ahead

b) School zone ahead

c) No parking zone

d) Railroad crossing ahead

Answer: a) Construction zone ahead

11. Question: What does a solid white line at an intersection indicate?

a) You must stop and yield to oncoming traffic

b) You may proceed through the intersection without stopping

c) You must make a right turn at the intersection

d) You are not allowed to change lanes

Answer: b) You may proceed through the intersection without stopping

12. Question: What is the purpose of an acceleration lane on a freeway?

a) To exit the freeway

b) To slow down before merging with traffic

c) To speed up and merge with traffic

d) To park your vehicle temporarily

Answer: c) To speed up and merge with traffic

13. Question: When are you required to use your turn signals?

a) Only when changing lanes

b) Only when making a right turn

c) Only when making a left turn

d) When changing lanes, making a left turn, or making a right turn

Answer: d) When changing lanes, making a left turn, or making a right turn

14. Question: What should you do if you miss your exit on a freeway?

a) Make a U-turn and go back to the exit

b) Reverse on the freeway to reach the exit

c) Continue to the next exit and retrace your route

d) Stop on the shoulder and wait for assistance

Answer: c) Continue to the next exit and retrace your route

15. Question: When parking downhill with a curb, you should turn your front wheels:

a) Away from the curb

b) Toward the curb

c) Parallel to the curb

d) It doesn't matter

Answer: b) Toward the curb

16. Question: What should you do if you encounter a large animal on the roadway?

a) Honk your horn and continue driving

b) Slow down, be prepared to stop, and avoid sudden movements

c) Swerve to avoid the animal

d) Speed up and pass the animal quickly

Answer: b) Slow down, be prepared to stop, and avoid sudden movements

17. Question: What is the appropriate action when approaching a flashing yellow traffic signal?

a) Stop and wait for the signal to turn green

b) Proceed with caution

c) Speed up to clear the intersection quickly

d) Stop and treat it as a stop sign

Answer: b) Proceed with caution

18. Question: When should you use your vehicle's hazard lights?

a) When parking in a no-parking zone

b) When driving in heavy rain or fog

c) When approaching a railroad crossing

d) When changing lanes on a freeway

Answer: b) When driving in heavy rain or fog

19. Question: What is the purpose of a car seatbelt?

a) To prevent the vehicle from rolling over

b) To keep the driver's hands on the steering wheel

c) To hold the driver and passengers in place during a collision

d) To increase the vehicle's fuel efficiency

Answer: c) To hold the driver and passengers in place during a collision

20. Question: What is the best way to handle a tire blowout?

a) Slam on the brakes to stop the vehicle immediately

b) Steer sharply to the side of the road

c) Grip the steering wheel firmly, ease off the accelerator, and gradually slow down

d) Accelerate to maintain control of the vehicle

21. Question: What is the best way to handle a tire blowout?

a) Slam on the brakes to stop the vehicle immediately

b) Steer sharply to the side of the road

c) Grip the steering wheel firmly, ease off the accelerator, and gradually slow down

d) Accelerate to maintain control of the vehicle

Answer: c) Grip the steering wheel firmly, ease off the accelerator, and gradually slow down

Question: What does a white rectangular sign with red lettering indicate?

a) Stop sign ahead

b) Yield sign ahead

c) Speed limit sign

d) Regulatory instruction or prohibition

Answer: d) Regulatory instruction or prohibition

22. Question: What should you do if your brakes fail while driving?

a) Pump the brakes rapidly

b) Shift into neutral and turn off the engine

c) Apply the parking brake gradually

d) Downshift to a lower gear and use engine braking

Answer: d) Downshift to a lower gear and use engine braking

23. Question: What is the purpose of a crosswalk?

a) To provide a safe path for pedestrians to cross the road

b) To indicate a parking area for vehicles

c) To designate a bicycle lane

d) To warn drivers of a railroad crossing ahead

Answer: a) To provide a safe path for pedestrians to cross the road

24. Question: What is the meaning of a solid red arrow at a traffic signal?

a) Stop and wait for the green arrow

b) Proceed in the direction of the arrow without stopping

c) Treat it as a yield sign

d) Make a U-turn if safe

Answer: a) Stop and wait for the green arrow

25. Question: What should you do if your vehicle's accelerator pedal becomes stuck?

a) Turn off the engine and use the brakes to slow down and stop

b) Shift into neutral and use the brakes to slow down and stop

c) Turn on the hazard lights and continue driving to the nearest service station

d) Pump the accelerator pedal to release it

Answer: b) Shift into neutral and use the brakes to slow down and stop

26. Question: What does a green arrow signal indicate?

a) Proceed in the direction of the arrow, but yield to other vehicles and pedestrians

b) Stop and wait for the green light

c) Make a U-turn if safe

d) No specific meaning

Answer: a) Proceed in the direction of the arrow, but yield to other vehicles and pedestrians

27. Question: When approaching a bicyclist on the road, what should you do?

a) Honk your horn to alert the bicyclist of your presence

b) Pass the bicyclist as closely as possible

c) Slow down and give the bicyclist ample space when passing

d) Drive in the bicycle lane to avoid the bicyclist

Answer: c) Slow down and give the bicyclist ample space when passing

28. Question: What is the purpose of a center lane with double yellow lines on each side?

a) To allow vehicles to make left turns from either direction

b) To provide an additional lane for passing slower vehicles

c) To designate a lane for bicycles only

d) To indicate a merging lane

Answer: a) To allow vehicles to make left turns from either direction

29. Question: When can you make a left turn at a red traffic light?

a) Never, unless a sign permits it

b) Only when there are no other vehicles present

c) Only when turning onto a one-way street from another one-way street

d) Only when turning onto a divided highway

Answer: c) Only when turning onto a one-way street from another one-way street

30. Question: What should you do if your vehicle starts to skid?

a) Steer in the direction you want the vehicle to go

b) Slam on the brakes to regain control

c) Accelerate to regain traction

d) Turn the steering wheel sharply in the opposite direction

Answer: a) Steer in the direction you want the vehicle to go

31. Question: When are you required to yield the right-of-way to pedestrians?

a) Only when they are crossing at a marked crosswalk

b) Only when they are crossing at an unmarked crosswalk

c) At all times, regardless of the presence of marked or unmarked crosswalks

d) Only when they are crossing at a traffic signal

Answer: c) At all times, regardless of the presence of marked or unmarked crosswalks

32. Question: What is the purpose of a diamond-shaped sign with an orange background?

a) To warn drivers of a school zone ahead

b) To indicate a construction or work zone

c) To guide drivers to a nearby hospital

d) To indicate a pedestrian crossing

Answer: b) To indicate a construction or work zone

33. Question: When approaching a railroad crossing with flashing red lights, you should:

a) Proceed with caution without stopping

b) Slow down and prepare to stop

c) Stop only if a train is visible

d) Stop and wait for the lights to stop flashing

Answer: d) Stop and wait for the lights to stop flashing

34. Question: What should you do if you are driving and feel drowsy or fatigued?

a) Increase your speed to stay alert

b) Open the window and turn up the radio volume

c) Pull over to a safe location and rest

d) Drink coffee or energy drinks to stay awake

Answer: c) Pull over to a safe location and rest

35. Question: When are you allowed to use your vehicle's high-beam headlights?

a) At all times to improve visibility

b) Only when driving on rural roads

c) Only when there are no other vehicles around

d) When driving in dimly lit areas and no oncoming vehicles are present

Answer: d) When driving in dimly lit areas and no oncoming vehicles are present

36. Question: What does a yellow diamond-shaped sign with black symbols indicate?

a) A construction zone ahead

b) An upcoming detour

c) A warning of potential hazards or dangerous conditions

d) A recommended speed limit for the area

Answer: c) A warning of potential hazards or dangerous conditions

37. Question: What should you do if your vehicle's headlights suddenly stop working at night?

a) Continue driving slowly with your hazard lights on

b) Turn on your high-beam headlights to compensate

c) Pull over to the side of the road and stop until the issue is resolved

d) Flash your high beams at oncoming vehicles to alert them

Answer: c) Pull over to the side of the road and stop until the issue is resolved

38. Question: When can you pass a vehicle on the right side?

a) Only when the vehicle in front is making a left turn

b) Only when there is a designated right-turn lane

c) Only on roads with more than one lane going in the same direction

d) Only when the vehicle in front is traveling below the speed limit

Answer: c) Only on roads with more than one lane going in the same direction

39. Question: What should you do if your vehicle's accelerator becomes stuck?

a) Shift into neutral and steer to a safe location

b) Pump the accelerator pedal rapidly to free it

c) Turn off the ignition and apply the brakes

d) Shift into a higher gear to slow down the vehicle

Answer: a) Shift into neutral and steer to a safe location

40. Question: When should you use your vehicle's horn?

a) To express frustration or annoyance at other drivers

b) To greet friends or acquaintances on the road

c) To warn others of a potential danger or to get their attention

d) Only when driving in residential areas

Answer: c) To warn others of a potential danger or to get their attention

41. Question: What is the recommended hand position on the steering wheel?

a) One hand at the top of the wheel

b) One hand at the bottom of the wheel

c) Both hands at the 10 and 2 o'clock positions

d) Both hands at the 9 and 3 o'clock positions

Answer: d) Both hands at the 9 and 3 o'clock positions

42. Question: When can you make a U-turn at an intersection?

a) Only at intersections with a "No U-turn" sign

b) Only at intersections controlled by traffic signals

c) Only at intersections with a designated U-turn lane

d) When there are no vehicles approaching from either direction

Answer: d) When there are no vehicles approaching from either direction

43. Question: What is the purpose of an HOV (High Occupancy Vehicle) lane?

a) To provide an extra lane for trucks and large vehicles

b) To allow only emergency vehicles to pass

c) To encourage carpooling by providing a lane for vehicles with multiple occupants

d) To indicate a merging lane for entering or exiting the highway

Answer: c) To encourage carpooling by providing a lane for vehicles with multiple occupants

44. Question: What should you do if you miss your intended exit on a highway?

a) Immediately back up to the missed exit

b) Continue driving until you find the next exit and turn around

c) Use the center median to make a U-turn and go back to the missed exit

d) Proceed to the next exit and re-route from there

Answer: d) Proceed to the next exit and re-route from there

45. Question: When parking uphill with a curb, which way should you turn your vehicle's wheels?

a) Away from the curb

b) Towards the curb

c) It doesn't matter

d) Parallel to the curb

Answer: a) Away from the curb

46. Question: What should you do if you encounter a large animal crossing the road?

a) Honk your horn to scare it away

b) Speed up to pass the animal quickly

c) Brake firmly and be prepared to stop

d) Swerve to avoid the animal

Answer: c) Brake firmly and be prepared to stop

47. Question: What is the purpose of a car's blind spot?

a) To enhance visibility for the driver

b) To block the driver's view of other vehicles

c) To create an area where other vehicles cannot be seen in the mirrors

d) It serves no specific purpose

Answer: c) To create an area where other vehicles cannot be seen in the mirrors

48. Question: What is the maximum speed limit in residential areas unless otherwise posted?

a) 20 mph

b) 25 mph

c) 30 mph

d) 35 mph

Answer: b) 25 mph

49. Question: What does a solid yellow line on your side of the centerline indicate?

a) No passing allowed

b) Passing allowed with caution

c) Passing allowed if the road is clear

d) Passing allowed for vehicles traveling below the speed limit

Answer: a) No passing allowed

50. Question: What should you do when approaching a roundabout?

a) Come to a complete stop and yield to all traffic in the roundabout

b) Maintain your speed and merge into the roundabout when it's safe

c) Speed up to enter the roundabout before other vehicles

d) Turn on your hazard lights and proceed through the roundabout

Answer: b) Maintain your speed and merge into the roundabout when it's safe

51. Question: What is the purpose of a white rectangular sign with black lettering?

a) To indicate a stop sign ahead

b) To provide information about a nearby tourist attraction

c) To indicate a speed limit zone

d) To provide regulatory information or guidelines

Answer: d) To provide regulatory information or guidelines

52. Question: When can you legally use your vehicle's hazard lights?

a) When driving in heavy traffic to warn other drivers

b) When parked illegally for a short period of time

c) When driving in adverse weather conditions

d) When making a turn at an intersection

Answer: c) When driving in adverse weather conditions

53. Question: What should you do when approaching a yield sign?

a) Come to a complete stop and proceed when the intersection is clear

b) Maintain your speed and yield to vehicles already in the intersection

c) Speed up to merge into traffic

d) Sound your horn to alert other drivers

Answer: a) Come to a complete stop and proceed when the intersection is clear

54. Question: What should you do if your vehicle's brakes fail?

a) Shift into neutral and use the emergency brake to slow down

b) Pump the brakes rapidly to restore brake pressure

c) Turn off the ignition and coast to a stop

d) Look for an open space to drive off the road and use friction to slow down

Answer: a) Shift into neutral and use the emergency brake to slow down

55. Question: What should you do if you are involved in a minor traffic collision with no injuries?

a) Exchange insurance information with the other party and report the incident to the police

b) Leave the scene immediately if there is no visible damage

c) Take photos of the damage and proceed to your destination

d) Apologize to the other party and admit fault

Answer: a) Exchange insurance information with the other party and report the incident to the police

56. Question: What is the purpose of a center turn lane?

a) To provide an extra lane for passing slower vehicles

b) To provide a lane for left turns from either direction

c) To serve as a merging lane when entering a highway

d) To provide a lane for right turns only

Answer: b) To provide a lane for left turns from either direction

57. Question: When should you use your vehicle's parking lights?

a) When driving in foggy conditions to increase visibility

b) When parked illegally for a short period of time

c) When parked on a hill or incline

d) When driving at night and parked off the roadway

Answer: d) When driving at night and parked off the roadway

58. Question: What does a green arrow signal mean?

a) Proceed with caution

b) Stop and yield to oncoming traffic

c) Make a protected turn in the direction of the arrow

d) Merge into the lane indicated by the arrow

Answer: c) Make a protected turn in the direction of the arrow

59. Question: What should you do if your vehicle's accelerator becomes stuck?

a) Shift into neutral and steer to a safe location

b) Pump the accelerator pedal rapidly to free it

c) Turn off the ignition and apply the brakes

d) Shift into a higher gear to slow down the vehicle

Answer: a) Shift into neutral and steer to a safe location

60. Question: What should you do if you encounter a school bus with its red lights flashing and stop sign extended?

a) Slow down and proceed with caution

b) Pass the school bus carefully on the left side

c) Stop and remain stopped until the lights stop flashing and the stop sign is retracted

d) Honk your horn to alert the bus driver

Answer: c) Stop and remain stopped until the lights stop flashing and the stop sign is retracted

61. Question: When can you legally pass another vehicle on the right side?

a) When the vehicle ahead is making a left turn

b) When there is a designated right-turn lane

c) When there are three or more lanes in your direction of travel

d) When the vehicle ahead is driving below the speed limit

Answer: a) When the vehicle ahead is making a left turn

62. Question: What should you do if your vehicle's tire blows out while driving?

a) Slam on the brakes to bring the vehicle to a stop

b) Steer sharply to the side of the road and come to a stop

c) Accelerate to maintain control of the vehicle

d) Maintain a firm grip on the steering wheel and gradually reduce speed

Answer: d) Maintain a firm grip on the steering wheel and gradually reduce speed

63. Question: What should you do when approaching a flashing yellow traffic signal?

a) Stop and wait for the signal to turn green

b) Proceed through the intersection without stopping

c) Slow down and proceed with caution

d) Make a left turn if it's safe to do so

Answer: c) Slow down and proceed with caution

64. Question: What is the purpose of an anti-lock braking system (ABS)?

a) To prevent the wheels from locking up during hard braking

b) To provide better fuel efficiency

c) To increase the maximum speed of the vehicle

d) To improve the vehicle's suspension system

Answer: a) To prevent the wheels from locking up during hard braking

65. Question: When should you use your vehicle's high beam headlights?

a) When driving in foggy conditions

b) When driving in well-lit urban areas

c) When approaching or following another vehicle closely

d) When driving on dark, unlit roads with no oncoming traffic

Answer: d) When driving on dark, unlit roads with no oncoming traffic

66. Question: What should you do if you are being tailgated by another vehicle?

a) Increase your speed to create more distance between your vehicles

b) Brake suddenly to discourage the tailgater from following closely

c) Move to a different lane if possible and allow the tailgater to pass

d) Ignore the tailgater and continue driving at your current speed

Answer: c) Move to a different lane if possible and allow the tailgater to pass

67. Question: What should you do if you miss your exit on a highway?

a) Immediately stop and back up to the missed exit

b) Continue driving until you find a safe opportunity to turn around

c) Make a U-turn at the next intersection to go back to the missed exit

d) Pull over to the shoulder and wait for assistance

Answer: b) Continue driving until you find a safe opportunity to turn around

68. Question: What does a solid white line on the road indicate?

a) No passing allowed

b) Passing allowed with caution

c) Passing allowed if the road is clear

d) Passing allowed for vehicles traveling below the speed limit

Answer: a) No passing allowed

69. Question: What is the purpose of a rumble strip on the side of the road?

a) To provide a smoother surface for driving

b) To alert drivers who drift out of their lane

c) To indicate a pedestrian crossing ahead

d) To mark the edge of the roadway

Answer: b) To alert drivers who drift out of their lane

70. Question: What should you do if you are approaching a large animal, such as a deer, on the road?

a) Flash your high beam headlights to scare the animal away

b) Swerve to avoid hitting the animal

c) Brake firmly and attempt to stop before reaching the animal

d) Slow down and be prepared to stop, as the animal may unexpectedly move into your path

Answer: d) Slow down and be prepared to stop, as the animal may unexpectedly move into your path

71. Question: When can you legally pass a vehicle on the right side using an unpaved shoulder?

a) When the vehicle ahead is driving below the speed limit

b) When there is a designated right-turn lane

c) When the vehicle ahead is making a left turn

d) When there is an obstruction in the roadway

Answer: d) When there is an obstruction in the roadway

72. Question: What should you do if you encounter a bicyclist on the road?

a) Honk your horn to alert the bicyclist of your presence

b) Drive as closely to the bicyclist as possible to provide more room for other vehicles

c) Slow down and give the bicyclist at least 3 feet of clearance when passing

d) Overtake the bicyclist as quickly as possible to avoid slowing down traffic

Answer: c) Slow down and give the bicyclist at least 3 feet of clearance when passing

73. Question: What is the purpose of a yellow

diamond-shaped sign with black symbols or lettering?

a) To indicate a school zone ahead

b) To provide information about nearby parking facilities

c) To indicate a railroad crossing ahead

d) To indicate a construction zone ahead

Answer: d) To indicate a construction zone ahead

74. Question: What should you do if your vehicle begins to hydroplane on a wet road?

a) Apply the brakes firmly to regain control of the vehicle

b) Steer sharply in the opposite direction of the skid

c) Take your foot off the accelerator and steer straight until you regain traction

d) Accelerate to try to get out of the hydroplane

Answer: c) Take your foot off the accelerator and steer straight until you regain traction

75. Question: What should you do if you are approaching a stopped school bus with its red lights flashing and stop sign extended on a divided highway?

a) Stop and remain stopped until the bus retracts its stop sign and turns off its red lights

b) Slow down and proceed with caution, as you are not required to stop on a divided highway

c) Stop only if there are children crossing the road

d) Pass the school bus carefully on the left side

Answer: a) Stop and remain stopped until the bus retracts its stop sign and turns off its red lights

76. Question: What should you do if you encounter a funeral procession while driving?

a) Honk your horn to indicate your presence to the procession

b) Drive between the vehicles in the procession to reach your destination more quickly

c) Yield the right-of-way to the procession and follow any instructions from law enforcement or funeral escorts

d) Pass the procession at a high rate of speed to avoid slowing down

Answer: c) Yield the right-of-way to the procession and follow any instructions from law enforcement or funeral escorts

77. Question: What should you do if your vehicle's engine suddenly overheats while driving?

a) Keep driving until you reach your destination and then turn off the engine

b) Immediately pull over to the side of the road and turn off the engine

c) Open the windows and turn on the air conditioning to cool down the engine

d) Add water to the radiator while the engine is still running

Answer: b) Immediately pull over to the side of the road and turn off the engine

78. Question: What does a yellow diamond-shaped sign with a black arrow pointing left indicate?

a) Right turn only ahead

b) Left turn only ahead

c) Merge left ahead

d) Lane shift to the left ahead

Answer: b) Left turn only ahead

79. Question: What should you do if your vehicle's accelerator pedal becomes stuck?

a) Apply the brakes firmly and shift into neutral

b) Pump the accelerator pedal to loosen it

c) Turn off the ignition and coast to a stop

d) Continuously press the accelerator pedal to try to free it

Answer: a) Apply the brakes firmly and shift into neutral

80. Question: What is the purpose of a traffic circle or roundabout?

a) To increase the maximum speed limit of the roadway

b) To provide a designated area for pedestrians to cross the road

c) To control the flow of traffic and reduce the risk of collisions

d) To allow vehicles to pass each other on narrow roads

Answer: c) To control the flow of traffic and reduce the risk of collisions

81. Question: When can you legally make a U-turn on a city street?

a) At any intersection with a traffic light

b) Only at intersections with a designated U-turn lane

c) When there are no vehicles approaching within 200 feet

d) Only if there is a "No U-turn" sign present

Answer: c) When there are no vehicles approaching within 200 feet

82. Question: What should you do if you miss your intended highway exit?

a) Immediately stop and reverse to the missed exit

b) Continue driving and take the next available exit

c) Make a U-turn at the next opportunity to go back to the missed exit

d) Pull over to the shoulder and wait for assistance

Answer: b) Continue driving and take the next available exit

83. Question: What does a red and white triangular sign indicate?

a) Yield the right-of-way

b) Stop and remain stopped

c) Slow down and prepare to merge

d) Speed limit reduction ahead

Answer: a) Yield the right-of-way

84. Question: What should you do if your vehicle's brakes fail?

a) Pump the brakes rapidly to try to regain brake pressure

b) Apply the emergency or parking brake gradually

c) Shift into a lower gear to slow down the vehicle

d) Use friction against the curb or roadside to slow down the vehicle

Answer: d) Use friction against the curb or roadside to slow down the vehicle

85. Question: What should you do if you encounter a funeral procession while driving?

a) Honk your horn to indicate your presence to the procession

b) Drive between the vehicles in the procession to reach your destination more quickly

c) Yield the right-of-way to the procession and follow any instructions from law enforcement or funeral escorts

d) Pass the procession at a high rate of speed to avoid slowing down

Answer: c) Yield the right-of-way to the procession and follow any instructions from law enforcement or funeral escorts

86. Question: What should you do if you are approaching a roundabout?

a) Stop and yield to traffic in the roundabout

b) Speed up to merge with the traffic in the roundabout

c) Enter the roundabout without yielding if there is no oncoming traffic

d) Signal and yield to traffic in the roundabout before entering

Answer: d) Signal and yield to traffic in the roundabout before entering

87. Question: What should you do if you encounter a bicyclist at a roundabout?

a) Sound your horn to alert the bicyclist of your presence

b) Pass the bicyclist closely to avoid slowing down

c) Yield to the bicyclist and give them plenty of space

d) Ignore the bicyclist and continue through the roundabout

Answer: c) Yield to the bicyclist and give them plenty of space

88. Question: What does a red "X" sign above a lane indicate?

a) The lane is closed, and you should merge into another lane

b) The lane is reserved for emergency vehicles only

c) The lane is for high-occupancy vehicles only

d) The lane is an exit lane

Answer: a) The lane is closed, and you should merge into another lane

89. Question: What is the purpose of a crosswalk?

a) To provide a designated area for pedestrians to cross the road

b) To indicate a merge or lane shift ahead

c) To mark the edge of the roadway

d) To indicate a pedestrian-only zone

Answer: a) To provide a designated area for pedestrians to cross the road

90. Question: What should you do if you are approaching a work zone with flaggers directing traffic?

a) Ignore the flaggers and continue through the work zone at your normal speed

b) Slow down and follow the directions given by the flaggers

c) Honk your horn to get the attention of the flaggers

d) Proceed through the work zone without stopping

Answer: b) Slow down and follow the directions given by the flaggers

91. Question: What should you do if you approach a flashing red traffic signal?

a) Treat it as a stop sign and come to a complete stop before proceeding

b) Treat it as a yield sign and proceed with caution

c) Continue driving without stopping if there is no cross traffic

d) Slow down and proceed through the intersection without stopping

Answer: a) Treat it as a stop sign and come to a complete stop before proceeding

92. Question: What does a white rectangular sign with black lettering indicate?

a) The maximum speed limit on the roadway

b) The location of a nearby hospital

c) The direction to a tourist attraction

d) Regulatory information or instructions

Answer: d) Regulatory information or instructions

93. Question: What should you do if you are driving and encounter dense fog?

a) Turn on your high beam headlights to improve visibility

b) Slow down, use your low beam headlights, and increase your following distance

c) Speed up to get out of the fog as quickly as possible

d) Stop your vehicle and wait for the fog to clear

Answer: b) Slow down, use your low beam headlights, and increase your following distance

94. Question: What is the purpose of rumble strips on the side of the road?

a) To indicate the presence of a pedestrian crossing

b) To warn drivers of a sharp curve ahead

c) To alert drivers if they are drifting out of their lane

d) To indicate the location of a bicycle lane

Answer: c) To alert drivers if they are drifting out of their lane

95. Question: What should you do if you are driving and a tire blows out?

a) Immediately apply the brakes to stop the vehicle

b) Steer sharply in the opposite direction of the blown tire

c) Gradually release the accelerator and steer straight until you regain control

d) Pump the brakes rapidly to regain control of the vehicle

Answer: c) Gradually release the accelerator and steer straight until you regain control

96. Question: What should you do if you are driving and encounter a flashing yellow traffic signal?

a) Come to a complete stop and wait for the signal to turn green

b) Slow down and proceed through the intersection with caution

c) Yield to any oncoming traffic before proceeding

d) Ignore the signal and continue driving at your normal speed

Answer: b) Slow down and proceed through the intersection with caution

97. Question: What does a solid yellow line on your side of the center divider indicate?

a) No passing allowed

b) Passing allowed if it is safe to do so

c) Passing allowed only during daylight hours

d) Passing allowed if you are driving a larger vehicle

Answer: a) No passing allowed

98. Question: What should you do if you are driving and encounter a bicyclist on a narrow roadway?

a) Honk your horn to alert the bicyclist of your presence

b) Pass the bicyclist closely to avoid slowing down

c) Slow down and wait for a safe opportunity to pass, giving the bicyclist ample space

d) Speed up to quickly pass the bicyclist and avoid slowing down traffic

Answer: c) Slow down and wait for a safe opportunity to pass, giving the bicyclist ample space

99. Question: What is the purpose of a diamond-shaped sign with a picture of a person walking?

a) To indicate a pedestrian-only zone

b) To indicate a crosswalk ahead

c) To mark the edge of the roadway

d) To warn drivers of a nearby school zone

Answer: b) To indicate a crosswalk ahead

100. Question: What should you do if you are driving and your vehicle's engine starts to overheat?

a) Turn off the engine and wait for it to cool down before continuing

b) Increase your speed to try to cool down the engine

c) Turn on the heater to help cool down the engine

d) Pull over to a safe location and allow the engine to cool down

Answer: d) Pull over to a safe location and allow the engine to cool down

101. Question: When are you required to use your headlights?

a) Only during nighttime hours

b) Only in inclement weather conditions

c) Whenever you have difficulty seeing other vehicles or objects on the road

d) Only in residential areas

Answer: c) Whenever you have difficulty seeing other vehicles or objects on the road

102. Question: What is the purpose of an HOV lane?

a) To provide additional space for parked vehicles

b) To separate different types of vehicles on the roadway

c) To provide a designated lane for high-occupancy vehicles

d) To indicate the presence of a bicycle lane

Answer: c) To provide a designated lane for high-occupancy vehicles

103. Question: What should you do if you are approaching a bicyclist from behind?

a) Honk your horn to let them know you're behind them

b) Pass them closely to avoid slowing down

c) Slow down and give them at least three feet of space when passing

d) Ignore them and continue driving at your normal speed

Answer: c) Slow down and give them at least three feet of space when passing

104. Question: What should you do if you are driving and your vehicle starts to skid?

a) Slam on the brakes to stop the skid

b) Steer in the opposite direction of the skid

c) Continue to apply the brakes firmly until the skid stops

d) Ease off the accelerator and steer in the direction you want to go

Answer: d) Ease off the accelerator and steer in the direction you want to go

105. Question: What is the maximum speed limit in a residential area, unless otherwise posted?

a) 25 mph

b) 35 mph

c) 45 mph

d) 55 mph

Answer: a) 25 mph

106. Question: What should you do if you are driving and encounter a flashing yellow arrow traffic signal?

a) Turn in the direction of the arrow without yielding

b) Treat it as a yield sign and proceed with caution

c) Stop and wait for the signal to turn green

d) Ignore the signal and continue driving at your normal speed

Answer: b) Treat it as a yield sign and proceed with caution

107. Question: What should you do if you are driving

and your vehicle's accelerator becomes stuck?

a) Immediately turn off the ignition

b) Apply the brakes firmly and shift into neutral

c) Quickly pump the accelerator pedal to loosen it

d) Try to lift the accelerator pedal with your foot

Answer: b) Apply the brakes firmly and shift into neutral

108. Question: What does a solid white line on the roadway indicate?

a) No passing allowed

b) Passing allowed if it is safe to do so

c) Passing allowed only during daylight hours

d) Passing allowed if you are driving a larger vehicle

Answer: a) No passing allowed

109. Question: What should you do if you are driving and encounter a yellow "Yield" sign?

a) Come to a complete stop and wait for the signal to turn green

b) Slow down and yield the right-of-way to oncoming traffic

c) Proceed through the intersection without stopping

d) Speed up to quickly pass other vehicles

Answer: b) Slow down and yield the right-of-way to oncoming traffic

110. Question: What should you do if you are driving and your vehicle's headlights suddenly fail?

a) Turn on your hazard lights and continue driving

b) Keep driving, but reduce your speed and use the center line as a guide

c) Pull over to a safe location and try to fix the problem or call for assistance

d) Increase your speed to reach your destination faster

Answer: c) Pull over to a safe location and try to fix the problem or call for assistance

111. Question: What should you do if you approach a pedestrian crossing the street using a white cane or guide dog?

a) Honk your horn to alert them of your presence

b) Slow down and yield the right-of-way to the pedestrian

c) Pass them closely to avoid delaying traffic

d) Proceed without slowing down as they have the right-of-way

Answer: b) Slow down and yield the right-of-way to the pedestrian

112. Question: When should you use your turn signal?

a) Only when changing lanes

b) Only when making a left turn

c) Only when making a right turn

d) Whenever you are changing direction or changing lanes

Answer: d) Whenever you are changing direction or changing lanes

113. Question: What is the purpose of a diamond-shaped sign with an arrow pointing downward?

a) To indicate a one-way road

b) To indicate a divided highway ahead

c) To indicate a construction zone

d) To indicate a detour or diversion

Answer: d) To indicate a detour or diversion

114. Question: What should you do if you are driving and your vehicle's brakes fail?

a) Pump the brakes quickly to try to regain pressure

b) Shift into a lower gear to slow down the vehicle

c) Use your emergency or parking brake to slow down the vehicle

d) Look for a safe area to steer off the roadway

Answer: c) Use your emergency or parking brake to slow down the vehicle

115. Question: What should you do if you are driving and encounter a funeral procession?

a) Pass the procession as quickly as possible

b) Drive at the speed limit and maintain your position in traffic

c) Yield the right-of-way to the procession and follow any instructions from law enforcement or funeral escorts

d) Honk your horn to show your respect for the deceased

Answer: c) Yield the right-of-way to the procession and follow any instructions from law enforcement or funeral escorts

116. Question: When should you use your hazard lights?

a) When driving in heavy traffic

b) When you need to make a sudden stop

c) When your vehicle is disabled or stopped on the roadway

d) When you want to warn other drivers of your presence

Answer: c) When your vehicle is disabled or stopped on the roadway

117. Question: What is the purpose of a white rectangular sign with black lettering and an arrow pointing downward?

a) To indicate a sharp turn ahead

b) To indicate a one-way road

c) To indicate a pedestrian crossing

d) To indicate a school zone

Answer: b) To indicate a one-way road

118. Question: What should you do if you are driving and encounter a funeral procession?

a) Pass the procession as quickly as possible

b) Drive at the speed limit and maintain your position in traffic

c) Yield the right-of-way to the procession and follow any instructions from law enforcement or funeral escorts

d) Honk your horn to show your respect for the deceased

Answer: c) Yield the right-of-way to the procession and follow any instructions from law enforcement or funeral escorts

119. Question: When are you required to stop for a school bus with its red lights flashing and stop sign extended?

a) Only if you are traveling in the opposite direction of the bus

b) Only if you are traveling in the same direction as the bus

c) Only if you are traveling on a two-lane road

d) In all directions, unless there is a physical barrier separating the lanes of traffic

Answer: d) In all directions, unless there is a physical barrier separating the lanes of traffic

120. Question: What is the purpose of a yellow diamond-shaped sign?

a) To indicate a school zone or crossing

b) To indicate a stop sign ahead

c) To indicate a pedestrian crossing

d) To indicate a railroad crossing

Answer: a) To indicate a school zone or crossing

121. Question: When parking uphill with a curb, which way should you turn your vehicle's wheels?

a) Away from the curb

b) Towards the curb

c) It doesn't matter

d) Parallel to the curb

Answer: a) Away from the curb

122. Question: What should you do if you are driving and encounter a bicyclist in a bike lane?

a) Honk your horn to let them know you're behind them

b) Drive in the bike lane to avoid slowing down

c) Give them plenty of space when passing and respect their right-of-way

d) Ignore them and continue driving at your normal speed

Answer: c) Give them plenty of space when passing and respect their right-of-way

123. Question: What should you do if you are driving and encounter a yellow traffic signal?

a) Speed up to quickly pass through the intersection

b) Slow down and proceed with caution

c) Come to a complete stop

d) Ignore the signal and continue driving at your normal speed

Answer: b) Slow down and proceed with caution

124. Question: When can you legally pass another vehicle on the right?

a) Only on one-way roads

b) Only when the vehicle in front is making a left turn

c) Only when there are two or more lanes traveling in the same direction

d) Only when the vehicle in front is driving below the speed limit

Answer: c) Only when there are two or more lanes traveling in the same direction

125. Question: What should you do if you are driving and encounter a flashing red traffic signal?

a) Proceed through the intersection without stopping

b) Treat it as a stop sign and come to a complete stop

c) Slow down and proceed with caution

d) Ignore the signal and continue driving at your normal speed

Answer: b) Treat it as a stop sign and come to a complete stop

126. Question: What should you do if you are driving and your vehicle's tire blows out?

a) Quickly turn the steering wheel in the opposite direction of the blowout

b) Slam on the brakes to stop the vehicle

c) Ease off the accelerator and grip the steering wheel firmly

d) Continue driving at your normal speed and seek assistance later

Answer: c) Ease off the accelerator and grip the steering wheel firmly

127. Question: What should you do if you are driving and encounter a solid yellow line on your side of the roadway?

a) Increase your speed to pass the vehicle in front of you

b) Slow down and prepare to stop

c) Yield to oncoming traffic and do not pass

d) Change lanes if it is safe to do so

Answer: c) Yield to oncoming traffic and do not pass

128. Question: What should you do if you are driving and your vehicle's headlights suddenly fail?

a) Turn on your hazard lights and continue driving

b) Keep driving, but reduce your speed and use the center line as a guide

c) Pull over to a safe location and try to fix the problem or call for assistance

d) Increase your speed to reach your destination faster

Answer: c) Pull over to a safe location and try to fix the problem or call for assistance

129. Question: What should you do if you are driving and encounter a pedestrian crossing the street outside of a marked crosswalk?

a) Yield the right-of-way and allow the pedestrian to cross

b) Honk your horn to warn the pedestrian

c) Continue driving without stopping

d) Speed up to pass the pedestrian quickly

Answer: a) Yield the right-of-way and allow the pedestrian to cross

130. Question: What should you do if you are driving and your vehicle starts to skid?

a) Slam on the brakes to stop the skid

b) Steer in the opposite direction of the skid

c) Take your foot off the accelerator and steer in the direction you want to go

d) Accelerate to regain control of the vehicle

Answer: c) Take your foot off the accelerator and steer in the direction you want to go

131. Question: When should you use your high beam headlights?

a) When driving in heavy traffic

b) When driving in foggy conditions

c) When driving in well-lit urban areas

d) When driving on an empty rural road

Answer: d) When driving on an empty rural road

132. Question: What is the purpose of a broken white line on the roadway?

a) To separate traffic moving in the same direction

b) To indicate a no passing zone

c) To mark the edge of the roadway

d) To indicate a construction zone

Answer: a) To separate traffic moving in the same direction

133. Question: What should you do if you are driving and a large truck is attempting to merge into your lane?

a) Speed up to pass the truck before it merges

b) Maintain your speed and position to allow the truck to merge safely

c) Honk your horn to let the truck driver know you're there

d) Change lanes to avoid the merging truck

Answer: b) Maintain your speed and position to allow the truck to merge safely

134. Question: When should you use your low beam headlights?

a) When driving in well-lit urban areas

b) When driving in foggy conditions

c) When driving on a dark road with no other vehicles around

d) When driving on a well-lit highway

Answer: a) When driving in well-lit urban areas

135. Question: What should you do if you are driving and a school bus with flashing red lights stops ahead of you?

a) Slow down and pass the bus cautiously

b) Stop at least 20 feet away from the bus and remain stopped until the lights stop flashing

c) Pass the bus quickly to avoid delay

d) Honk your horn to let the bus driver know you're waiting

Answer: b) Stop at least 20 feet away from the bus and remain stopped until the lights stop flashing

136. Question: What should you do if you are driving and a bicyclist is using a hand signal to indicate a left turn?

a) Ignore the hand signal and continue driving

b) Speed up to pass the bicyclist before they turn

c) Slow down and yield the right-of-way to the bicyclist

d) Honk your horn to let the bicyclist know you're there

Answer: c) Slow down and yield the right-of-way to the bicyclist

137. Question: What should you do if you are driving and your vehicle's accelerator pedal becomes stuck?

a) Quickly turn off the ignition to stop the vehicle

b) Shift into neutral and use the brakes to slow down and stop the vehicle

c) Slam on the brakes to try to unstick the accelerator

d) Continuously pump the accelerator pedal to unstick it

Answer: b) Shift into neutral and use the brakes to slow down and stop the vehicle

138. Question: What should you do if you are driving

and your vehicle's power steering fails?

a) Use extra force to turn the steering wheel

b) Slow down and pull off the roadway to a safe location

c) Continuously turn the steering wheel back and forth to regain control

d) Use your emergency lights to signal other drivers

Answer: b) Slow down and pull off the roadway to a safe location

139. Question: What should you do if you are driving and a tire blows out?

a) Slam on the brakes to stop the vehicle

b) Steer in the opposite direction of the blowout

c) Ease off the accelerator and grip the steering wheel firmly

d) Continue driving at your normal speed

Answer: c) Ease off the accelerator and grip the steering wheel firmly

140. Question: What should you do if you are driving and your vehicle's brakes fail?

a) Pump the brakes to build up pressure

b) Use the emergency/parking brake to slow down and stop the vehicle

c) Continuously honk your horn to warn other drivers

d) Change lanes quickly to avoid potential collisions

Answer: b) Use the emergency/parking brake to slow down and stop the vehicle

141. Question: What is the purpose of an acceleration lane on a freeway?

a) To slow down and prepare for exiting the freeway

b) To merge safely into the flow of traffic

c) To park your vehicle temporarily

d) To pass slower vehicles on the freeway

Answer: b) To merge safely into the flow of traffic

142. Question: When approaching a railroad crossing with flashing red lights, you should:

a) Slow down and proceed with caution

b) Stop and wait for the lights to stop flashing

c) Increase your speed to quickly cross the tracks

d) Honk your horn to warn other drivers

Answer: b) Stop and wait for the lights to stop flashing

143. Question: If you are driving and your vehicle's engine overheats, you should:

a) Pour cold water on the engine to cool it down

b) Continue driving to your destination and have the engine checked later

c) Pull over to a safe location and turn off the engine

d) Increase your speed to create more air circulation

Answer: c) Pull over to a safe location and turn off the engine

144. Question: When can you legally pass a vehicle on the right side?

a) When the vehicle ahead is making a left turn

b) When the vehicle ahead is driving below the speed limit

c) When there is an open lane for passing

d) When the vehicle ahead is driving on a one-way street

Answer: a) When the vehicle ahead is making a left turn

145. Question: What should you do if you approach an intersection with a traffic signal that is not working?

a) Treat it as a stop sign and come to a complete stop

b) Proceed through the intersection without stopping

c) Speed up to quickly pass through the intersection

d) Ignore the signal and continue driving at your normal speed

Answer: a) Treat it as a stop sign and come to a complete stop

146. Question: What should you do if you are driving and your vehicle's headlights are not working properly at night?

a) Use your high beam headlights instead

b) Increase your speed to reach your destination faster

c) Pull over to a safe location and have the headlights checked

d) Continue driving, but reduce your speed

Answer: c) Pull over to a safe location and have the headlights checked

147. Question: When can you legally make a U-turn?

a) On a curve or near the top of a hill where other drivers cannot see you

b) In a residential area with heavy pedestrian traffic

c) In a business district during daylight hours

d) When there is a "No U-turn" sign posted

Answer: c) In a business district during daylight hours

148. Question: What should you do if you are driving and encounter a vehicle coming towards you with its high beam headlights on?

a) Flash your high beam headlights to signal the other driver

b) Look to the right side of the road to avoid being blinded

c) Slow down and pull over to the side until the vehicle passes

d) Turn on your high beam headlights in response

Answer: b) Look to the right side of the road to avoid being blinded

149. Question: What is the minimum following distance you should maintain behind the vehicle ahead of you?

a) 1 second

b) 2 seconds

c) 3 seconds

d) 4 seconds

Answer: c) 3 seconds

150. Question: What should you do if you are driving and a tire blows out?

a) Slam on the brakes to stop the vehicle

b) Steer in the opposite direction of the blowout

c) Ease off the accelerator and grip the steering wheel firmly

d) Continue driving at your normal speed

Answer: c) Ease off the accelerator and grip the steering wheel firmly

151. Question: What is the purpose of a diamond-shaped sign?

a) To indicate a railroad crossing

b) To indicate a stop sign ahead

c) To indicate a yield sign ahead

d) To indicate a school zone

Answer: a) To indicate a railroad crossing

152. Question: When should you use your hazard lights?

a) When driving in heavy traffic

b) When parked on the side of the road

c) When driving in foggy conditions

d) When passing another vehicle

Answer: b) When parked on the side of the road

153. Question: What does a solid yellow line on the roadway indicate?

a) No passing in either direction

b) Passing is allowed in both directions

c) Passing is allowed in one direction

d) Passing is allowed with caution

Answer: a) No passing in either direction

154. Question: What should you do if you are driving and a tire blows out?

a) Slam on the brakes to stop the vehicle

b) Steer in the opposite direction of the blowout

c) Ease off the accelerator and grip the steering wheel firmly

d) Continue driving at your normal speed

Answer: c) Ease off the accelerator and grip the steering wheel firmly

155. Question: What is the purpose of a roundabout?

a) To slow down traffic and reduce congestion

b) To allow for easy U-turns

c) To speed up traffic flow on a highway

d) To provide a designated area for parking

Answer: a) To slow down traffic and reduce congestion

156. Question: What should you do if you are driving and a pedestrian is

crossing the street using a crosswalk?

a) Slow down and yield the right-of-way to the pedestrian

b) Honk your horn to warn the pedestrian

c) Speed up to pass the pedestrian quickly

d) Continue driving without stopping

Answer: a) Slow down and yield the right-of-way to the pedestrian

157. Question: When should you use your turn signals?

a) Only when turning left

b) Only when turning right

c) Only when changing lanes

d) When turning or changing lanes

Answer: d) When turning or changing lanes

158. Question: What does a red traffic sign indicate?

a) Stop or prohibition

b) Caution or warning

c) Information or guidance

d) Direction or guidance

Answer: a) Stop or prohibition

159. Question: What should you do if you approach an intersection with a flashing red traffic signal?

a) Stop and proceed when safe

b) Slow down and proceed with caution

c) Treat it as a yield sign and proceed with caution

d) Ignore the signal and continue driving

Answer: a) Stop and proceed when safe

160. Question: What should you do if you are driving and a vehicle with a siren and flashing lights approaches from behind?

a) Speed up to get out of the way quickly

b) Pull over to the right side of the road and stop

c) Change lanes to the left to allow the vehicle to pass

d) Continue driving at your current speed

Answer: b) Pull over to the right side of the road and stop

161. Question: When should you use your headlights during the daytime?

a) Only in foggy or rainy conditions

b) Only when driving on a highway

c) Only when driving in residential areas

d) When visibility is significantly reduced

Answer: d) When visibility is significantly reduced

162. Question: What does a green arrow signal indicate?

a) Proceed with caution

b) Stop and yield to other vehicles

c) Make a U-turn

d) You have the right-of-way to turn

Answer: d) You have the right-of-way to turn

163. Question: When should you yield the right-of-way to pedestrians?

a) Only when they are crossing at a marked crosswalk

b) Only when they are crossing at an intersection

c) Always, regardless of where they are crossing

d) Only when there is a traffic signal for pedestrians

Answer: c) Always, regardless of where they are crossing

164. Question: What should you do when approaching a flashing yellow traffic signal?

a) Speed up and proceed quickly

b) Slow down and proceed with caution

c) Stop and wait for the signal to turn green

d) Change lanes to avoid the signal

Answer: b) Slow down and proceed with caution

165. Question: What is the purpose of a center lane marked with double yellow lines on both sides?

a) To allow vehicles to pass in either direction

b) To provide a dedicated lane for left turns

c) To designate a parking area for disabled vehicles

d) To separate opposing lanes of traffic

Answer: b) To provide a dedicated lane for left turns

166. Question: What should you do if you are driving and a tire blows out?

a) Steer in the opposite direction of the blowout

b) Brake abruptly to stop the vehicle

c) Accelerate to maintain control of the vehicle

d) Ease off the accelerator and maintain a firm grip on the steering wheel

Answer: d) Ease off the accelerator and maintain a firm grip on the steering wheel

167. Question: What should you do if you are driving and your brakes become wet?

a) Pump the brakes to dry them out

b) Increase your speed to dry the brakes faster

c) Pull over and wait for the brakes to dry

d) Apply gentle and consistent pressure to the brakes to dry them

Answer: d) Apply gentle and consistent pressure to the brakes to dry them

168. Question: What should you do if you are driving and your vehicle's accelerator becomes stuck?

a) Turn off the ignition to shut off the engine

b) Apply the parking brake to slow down and stop the vehicle

c) Shift into neutral and safely move to the side of the road

d) Quickly pump the accelerator to loosen it

Answer: c) Shift into neutral and safely move to the side of the road

169. Question: What does a yellow diamond-shaped sign with a black cross inside indicate?

a) Hospital ahead

b) School zone ahead

c) Construction zone ahead

d) Intersection ahead

Answer: b) School zone ahead

170. Question: What should you do if you approach a roundabout?

a) Speed up to quickly pass through the roundabout

b) Yield to traffic already in the roundabout

c) Honk your horn to signal your entry

d) Make a complete stop before entering the roundabout

Answer: b) Yield to traffic already in the roundabout

171. Question: What should you do if you are approaching a railroad crossing with flashing lights and gates?

a) Slow down and proceed with caution

b) Stop and wait for the lights and gates to deactivate

c) Change lanes to avoid the crossing

d) Speed up to quickly pass through the crossing

Answer: b) Stop and wait for the lights and gates to deactivate

172.   Question: What does a solid white line on the roadway indicate?

a) No passing in either direction

b) Passing is allowed in both directions

c) Passing is allowed in one direction

d) Passing is allowed with caution

Answer: a) No passing in either direction

173.   Question: What is the purpose of an HOV lane?

a) To allow for easy U-turns

b) To provide a designated area for parking

c) To speed up traffic flow for vehicles with multiple occupants

d) To slow down traffic and reduce congestion

Answer: c) To speed up traffic flow for vehicles with multiple occupants

174.   Question: When should you use your high-beam headlights?

a) When driving in residential areas

b) When driving in foggy conditions

c) When driving on a well-lit highway

d) When driving on dark roads with no other vehicles nearby

Answer: d) When driving on dark roads with no other vehicles nearby

175. Question: What does a broken white line on the roadway indicate?

a) No passing in either direction

b) Passing is allowed in both directions

c) Passing is allowed in one direction

d) Passing is allowed with caution

Answer: b) Passing is allowed in both directions

176. Question: What should you do if you are approaching a school bus with its red lights flashing and stop sign extended?

a) Speed up and pass the school bus quickly

b) Stop and wait until the lights stop flashing and the stop sign is retracted

c) Slow down and proceed with caution

d) Change lanes to avoid the school bus

Answer: b) Stop and wait until the lights stop flashing and the stop sign is retracted

177. Question: What does a white rectangular sign with black lettering indicate?

a) Stop sign ahead

b) Yield sign ahead

c) Speed limit sign

d) Information or guidance sign

Answer: d) Information or guidance sign

178. Question: What should you do if you miss your intended highway exit?

a) Continue driving until the next exit and turn around

b) Reverse on the highway to reach the missed exit

c) Pull over to the shoulder and wait for assistance

d) Proceed to the next exit and find an alternate route

Answer: d) Proceed to the next exit and find an alternate route

179. Question: What should you do if you encounter a bicyclist on the road?

a) Honk your horn to alert the bicyclist of your presence

b) Pass the bicyclist as closely as possible

c) Slow down and give the bicyclist ample space when passing

d) Ignore the bicyclist and continue driving

Answer: c) Slow down and give the bicyclist ample space when passing

180. Question: What should you do if you approach a flashing yellow arrow traffic signal?

a) Stop and wait for the signal to turn green

b) Proceed with caution, yielding to oncoming traffic

c) Treat it as a stop sign and come to a complete stop

d) Change lanes to avoid the signal

Answer: b) Proceed with caution, yielding to oncoming traffic

181. Question: What is the purpose of rumble strips on the roadway?

a) To provide a smoother driving surface

b) To alert drivers of upcoming construction zones

c) To prevent excessive speeding

d) To warn drivers of potential hazards or lane departures

Answer: d) To warn drivers of potential hazards or lane departures

182. Question: What does a yellow diamond-shaped sign with a black arrow pointing left indicate?

a) One-way road ahead

b) Merge left ahead

c) Left turn only ahead

d) Yield to oncoming traffic

Answer: c) Left turn only ahead

183. Question: What should you do if you are driving and encounter heavy rain or fog?

a) Turn on your hazard lights and continue driving at the same speed

b) Increase your speed to pass through the rain or fog quickly

c) Slow down, use your headlights, and increase your following distance

d) Pull over to the side of the road and wait for the rain or fog to subside

Answer: c) Slow down, use your headlights, and increase your following distance

184. Question: What is the purpose of a car seat or booster seat for children?

a) To provide extra comfort during long drives

b) To keep children occupied while driving

c) To help children see better out of the window

d) To provide proper restraint and protection in case of a collision

Answer: d) To provide proper restraint and protection in case of a collision

185. Question: What should you do if you are driving and a large commercial truck is attempting to merge into your lane?

a) Speed up to avoid being in the truck's blind spot

b) Maintain your speed and force the truck to yield

c) Slow down or change lanes to allow the truck to merge safely

d) Honk your horn to alert the truck driver of your presence

Answer: c) Slow down or change lanes to allow the truck to merge safely

186. Question: What does a solid yellow line alongside a broken yellow line indicate?

a) Passing is allowed in both directions

b) No passing in either direction

c) Passing is allowed in one direction

d) Passing is allowed with caution

Answer: c) Passing is allowed in one direction

187. Question: What should you do if your vehicle's accelerator becomes stuck while driving?

a) Turn off the ignition to shut off the engine

b) Apply the parking brake to slow down and stop the vehicle

c) Shift into neutral and safely move to the side of the road

d) Quickly pump the accelerator to loosen it

Answer: c) Shift into neutral and safely move to the side of the road

188. Question: What does a red circle with a white horizontal line indicate?

a) Stop sign ahead

b) No left turn allowed

c) No parking or standing allowed

d) No U-turn allowed

Answer: b) No left turn allowed

189. Question: What should you do if you are driving and your vehicle's tire blows out?

a) Steer in the opposite direction of the blowout

b) Brake abruptly to stop the vehicle

c) Accelerate to maintain control of the vehicle

d) Ease off the accelerator and maintain a firm grip on the steering wheel

Answer: d) Ease off the accelerator and maintain a firm grip on the steering wheel

190. Question: What should you do if you are driving and encounter a bicyclist who is signaling to make a right turn?

a) Pass the bicyclist on the right side

b) Speed up to get ahead of the bicyclist

c) Slow down and let the bicyclist complete the right turn

d) Honk your horn to alert the bicyclist

Answer: c) Slow down and let the bicyclist complete the right turn

191. Question: What does a white triangle-shaped sign with a red border and an exclamation mark indicate?

a) Construction zone ahead

b) Yield ahead

c) School zone ahead

d) Warning of a potential hazard ahead

Answer: d) Warning of a potential hazard ahead

192. Question: When should you use your turn signals while driving?

a) Only when you are changing lanes

b) Only when you are making a left turn

c) Only when you are making a right turn

d) When changing lanes, making a left turn, or making a right turn

Answer: d) When changing lanes, making a left turn, or making a right turn

c) To indicate the average speed of vehicles on the roadway

d) To indicate the speed at which you should accelerate

193. Question: What should you do if your vehicle's headlights are not working properly at night?

a) Continue driving without headlights

b) Use your high beams instead

c) Use your hazard lights instead

d) Pull over to the side of the road and have the headlights repaired

Answer: d) Pull over to the side of the road and have the headlights repaired

194. Question: What is the purpose of a speed limit sign?

a) To indicate the minimum speed allowed on the roadway

b) To indicate the maximum speed allowed on the roadway

Answer: b) To indicate the maximum speed allowed on the roadway

195. Question: What should you do if you are driving and a tire blows out?

a) Slam on the brakes to stop the vehicle quickly

b) Steer in the opposite direction of the blowout

c) Maintain your speed and continue driving

d) Ease off the accelerator and steer straight

Answer: d) Ease off the accelerator and steer straight

196. Question: What does a solid red traffic signal indicate?

a) Proceed with caution

b) Stop and wait for the signal to turn green

c) Change lanes to avoid the signal

d) Slow down and prepare to yield

Answer: b) Stop and wait for the signal to turn green

197. Question: What should you do if you are driving and your brakes fail?

a) Pump the brakes rapidly to regain pressure

b) Downshift to a lower gear to slow down the vehicle

c) Use the emergency/parking brake to gradually stop the vehicle

d) Steer off the road and into a soft surface to stop the vehicle

Answer: c) Use the emergency/parking brake to gradually stop the vehicle

198. Question: What does a rectangular sign with a white line through a red circle indicate?

a) Stop sign ahead

b) No entry or do not enter

c) No parking or standing allowed

d) No U-turn allowed

Answer: b) No entry or do not enter

199. Question: What should you do if you are driving and a pedestrian enters a crosswalk?

a) Speed up to get through the crosswalk quickly

b) Yield the right-of-way to the pedestrian

c) Honk your horn to alert the pedestrian

d) Change lanes to avoid the crosswalk

Answer: b) Yield the right-of-way to the pedestrian

200. Question: What should you do if you are driving and your vehicle's

accelerator becomes stuck?

a) Turn off the ignition to shut off the engine

b) Apply the parking brake to slow down and stop the vehicle

c) Shift into neutral and safely move to the side of the road

d) Quickly pump the accelerator to loosen it

Answer: c) Shift into neutral and safely move to the side of the road

201. Question: What does a white rectangular sign with black lettering and a red circle indicate?

a) Speed limit ahead

b) No parking or standing allowed

c) No passing zone

d) Yield ahead

Answer: c) No passing zone

202. Question: When should you use your hazard lights while driving?

a) When you are double-parked

b) When you are driving in heavy rain

c) When you are driving in foggy conditions

d) When you are stopped or disabled on the roadway

Answer: d) When you are stopped or disabled on the roadway

203. Question: What should you do if you are driving and your vehicle's engine overheats?

a) Turn off the engine and wait for it to cool down

b) Open the hood to let the heat escape

c) Pour cold water on the engine to cool it down quickly

d) Keep driving and ignore the issue

Answer: a) Turn off the engine and wait for it to cool down

204. Question: What should you do if you are driving

and your vehicle's wheels start to skid?

a) Steer in the direction of the skid

b) Slam on the brakes to stop the skid

c) Steer in the opposite direction of the skid

d) Maintain your steering and apply steady pressure to the brakes

Answer: a) Steer in the direction of the skid

205. Question: What does a yellow diamond-shaped sign with black symbols or words indicate?

a) School zone ahead

b) Construction zone ahead

c) Pedestrian crossing ahead

d) Warning of a potential hazard ahead

Answer: d) Warning of a potential hazard ahead

206. Question: What should you do if you are driving

and your vehicle's tire blows out?

a) Slam on the brakes to stop the vehicle

b) Steer in the opposite direction of the blowout

c) Accelerate to maintain control of the vehicle

d) Ease off the accelerator and maintain a firm grip on the steering wheel

Answer: d) Ease off the accelerator and maintain a firm grip on the steering wheel

207. Question: What should you do if you are driving and a bicyclist is riding in front of you?

a) Honk your horn to alert the bicyclist of your presence

b) Drive as close to the bicyclist as possible to pass

c) Slow down and give the bicyclist at least 3 feet of space

d) Pass the bicyclist at high speed

Answer: c) Slow down and give the bicyclist at least 3 feet of space

208. Question: What does a red triangle-shaped sign indicate?

a) Yield ahead

b) Stop sign ahead

c) No right turn allowed

d) Warning of a potential hazard ahead

Answer: d) Warning of a potential hazard ahead

209. Question: What should you do if you are driving and encounter a flashing yellow traffic signal?

a) Stop and wait for the signal to turn green

b) Slow down and proceed with caution

c) Speed up to clear the intersection quickly

d) Come to a complete stop and yield to oncoming traffic

Answer: b) Slow down and proceed with caution

210. Question: What should you do if you are driving and your vehicle's brakes fail?

a) Pump the brakes rapidly to regain pressure

b) Downshift to a lower gear to slow down the vehicle

c) Use the emergency/parking brake to gradually stop the vehicle

d) Steer off the road and into a soft surface to stop the vehicle

Answer: c) Use the emergency/parking brake to gradually stop the vehicle

211. Question: When are you required to use your headlights while driving?

a) Only during nighttime

b) Only during inclement weather

c) Only when visibility is less than 500 feet

d) During nighttime, inclement weather, and when visibility is less than 500 feet

Answer: d) During nighttime, inclement weather, and when visibility is less than 500 feet

212. Question: What does a green traffic signal indicate?

a) Stop and wait for the signal to turn red

b) Proceed with caution

c) Yield to oncoming traffic

d) Proceed when it is safe to do so

Answer: d) Proceed when it is safe to do so

213. Question: What should you do if you are driving and a tire blows out?

a) Slam on the brakes to stop the vehicle quickly

b) Steer in the opposite direction of the blowout

c) Maintain your speed and continue driving

d) Ease off the accelerator and steer straight

Answer: d) Ease off the accelerator and steer straight

214. Question: What should you do if you approach a school bus with its red lights flashing and stop sign extended?

a) Pass the school bus carefully on the left side

b) Stop and wait until the bus resumes motion or the lights stop flashing

c) Slow down and proceed with caution without stopping

d) Honk your horn to alert the bus driver

Answer: b) Stop and wait until the bus resumes motion or the lights stop flashing

215. Question: What does a solid yellow traffic signal indicate?

a) Proceed with caution

b) Stop and wait for the signal to turn green

c) Change lanes to avoid the signal

d) Slow down and prepare to stop

Answer: d) Slow down and prepare to stop

216. Question: What should you do if you are driving and your vehicle's accelerator becomes stuck?

a) Turn off the ignition to shut off the engine

b) Apply the parking brake to slow down and stop the vehicle

c) Shift into neutral and safely move to the side of the road

d) Quickly pump the accelerator to loosen it

Answer: c) Shift into neutral and safely move to the side of the road

217. Question: When can you pass a vehicle on the right side?

a) When the vehicle is signaling a right turn

b) When the vehicle is traveling below the speed limit

c) When there is a designated lane for passing on the right

d) Passing on the right is not allowed unless in a specific situation

Answer: c) When there is a designated lane for passing on the right

218. Question: What should you do if you are driving and a pedestrian is crossing the street at a marked crosswalk?

a) Speed up to get through the crosswalk quickly

b) Yield the right-of-way to the pedestrian

c) Honk your horn to alert the pedestrian

d) Change lanes to avoid the crosswalk

Answer: b) Yield the right-of-way to the pedestrian

219. Question: What does a rectangular sign with a black line through a red circle indicate?

a) Stop sign ahead

b) No entry or do not enter

c) No parking or standing allowed

d) No U-turn allowed

c) Warning of a potential hazard ahead

d) Pedestrian crossing ahead

Answer: b) No entry or do not enter

220. Question: What should you do if you are driving and a bicyclist is riding on the right side of the road?

a) Honk your horn to alert the bicyclist of your presence

b) Pass the bicyclist closely to save time

c) Slow down and give the bicyclist at least 3 feet of space

d) Speed up to get past the bicyclist quickly

Answer: c) Slow down and give the bicyclist at least 3 feet of space

221. Question: What does a yellow triangle-shaped sign with an exclamation mark inside indicate?

a) Yield ahead

b) No passing zone

Answer: c) Warning of a potential hazard ahead

222. Question: What should you do when approaching a railroad crossing with flashing lights and gates down?

a) Proceed with caution and drive around the gates if no train is visible

b) Stop before the crossing and wait for the train to pass

c) Slow down and continue driving if no train is approaching

d) Speed up to clear the tracks quickly

Answer: b) Stop before the crossing and wait for the train to pass

223. Question: When should you use your high-beam headlights while driving?

a) In foggy conditions to increase visibility

b) When approaching oncoming traffic

c) When driving on well-lit city streets

d) When driving on dark, unlit roads

Answer: d) When driving on dark, unlit roads

224. Question: What should you do if you are driving and your vehicle starts to hydroplane on a wet road?

a) Slam on the brakes to regain control

b) Steer in the opposite direction of the skid

c) Ease off the accelerator and steer straight

d) Accelerate to maintain control of the vehicle

Answer: c) Ease off the accelerator and steer straight

225. Question: What does a blue circular sign with a white arrow indicate?

a) Right turn only

b) Left turn only

c) One-way traffic

d) Mandatory roundabout ahead

Answer: c) One-way traffic

226. Question: What should you do if you are driving and a tire blows out?

a) Steer in the direction of the blowout

b) Steer in the opposite direction of the blowout

c) Apply the brakes abruptly to stop the vehicle

d) Maintain your steering and gradually slow down

Answer: d) Maintain your steering and gradually slow down

227. Question: What should you do if you approach a stopped school bus with its red lights flashing and stop sign extended, but you are on a divided highway?

a) Pass the bus cautiously on the left side

b) Stop and wait for the bus to resume motion or the lights to stop flashing

c) Proceed with caution without stopping

d) Honk your horn to alert the bus driver

b) Shift into a lower gear to slow down the vehicle

c) Use the emergency/parking brake to gradually stop the vehicle

d) Steer off the road and into a soft surface to stop the vehicle

Answer: b) Stop and wait for the bus to resume motion or the lights to stop flashing

Answer: c) Use the emergency/parking brake to gradually stop the vehicle

228. Question: What does a green arrow signal indicate?

a) Stop and wait for the signal to turn green

b) Proceed with caution

c) Make a protected turn in the direction of the arrow

d) Yield to oncoming traffic

Answer: c) Make a protected turn in the direction of the arrow

229. Question: What should you do if you are driving and your brakes fail?

a) Pump the brakes rapidly to regain pressure

230. Question: What should you do if you are driving and encounter a flashing yellow arrow signal?

a) Stop and wait for the signal to turn green

b) Proceed with caution after yielding to any pedestrians or vehicles

c) Make a U-turn if it is safe to do so

d) Prepare to make a left turn when the signal turns solid green

Answer: b) Proceed with caution after yielding to any pedestrians or vehicles

231. Question: What does a diamond-shaped sign with an orange background indicate?

a) Road work or construction zone ahead

b) School zone or crossing ahead

c) No passing zone

d) Stop sign ahead

Answer: a) Road work or construction zone ahead

232. Question: What should you do if you are driving and encounter a flashing red traffic signal?

a) Proceed with caution after yielding to any pedestrians or vehicles

b) Stop and wait for the signal to turn solid red

c) Treat it as a yield sign and proceed if the intersection is clear

d) Ignore the signal and continue driving

Answer: b) Stop and wait for the signal to turn solid red

233. Question: What should you do if you are driving and your vehicle's brakes become wet and less effective?

a) Pump the brakes rapidly to dry them out

b) Drive slowly and apply the brakes gently to dry them out

c) Shift into a lower gear to slow down the vehicle

d) Use the emergency/parking brake to slow down and stop

Answer: b) Drive slowly and apply the brakes gently to dry them out

234. Question: What does a yellow rectangular sign with two black arrows pointing in opposite directions indicate?

a) Two-way traffic ahead

b) Divided highway ends

c) Lane ends, merge with traffic

d) No passing zone

Answer: c) Lane ends, merge with traffic

235. Question: What should you do if you are driving and your vehicle's accelerator becomes stuck?

a) Shift into neutral and safely move to the side of the road

b) Turn off the ignition to shut off the engine

c) Apply the parking brake to slow down and stop the vehicle

d) Quickly pump the accelerator to loosen it

Answer: a) Shift into neutral and safely move to the side of the road

236. Question: What should you do if you are driving and encounter a bicyclist on the road?

a) Honk your horn to alert the bicyclist of your presence

b) Pass the bicyclist closely to save time

c) Slow down and give the bicyclist at least 3 feet of space

d) Speed up to get past the bicyclist quickly

Answer: c) Slow down and give the bicyclist at least 3 feet of space

237. Question: What does a white rectangular sign with black lettering indicate?

a) Speed limit ahead

b) School zone ahead

c) No parking zone

d) Stop sign ahead

Answer: c) No parking zone

238. Question: What should you do if you are driving and encounter a pedestrian using a white cane or guide dog?

a) Proceed with caution and yield the right-of-way to the pedestrian

b) Honk your horn to alert the pedestrian of your presence

c) Drive around the pedestrian to avoid delay

d) Speed up to get past the pedestrian quickly

Answer: a) Proceed with caution and yield the right-of-way to the pedestrian

239. Question: What does a red triangular sign with a white exclamation mark inside indicate?

a) Yield ahead

b) No passing zone

c) Warning of a potential hazard ahead

d) School zone ahead

Answer: c) Warning of a potential hazard ahead

240. Question: What should you do if you are driving and a tire blows out?

a) Steer in the direction of the blowout

b) Steer in the opposite direction of the blowout

c) Apply the brakes abruptly to stop the vehicle

d) Maintain your steering and gradually slow down

Answer: d) Maintain your steering and gradually slow down

241. Question: What does a yellow diamond-shaped sign with black symbols of a person and a bicycle indicate?

a) Bicycle parking area ahead

b) Bicycles prohibited in the area

c) Shared lane with bicycles ahead

d) Bicycles must yield to pedestrians ahead

Answer: c) Shared lane with bicycles ahead

242. Question: What should you do if you are driving and a tire blows out?

a) Slam on the brakes to regain control

b) Steer in the opposite direction of the blowout

c) Ease off the accelerator and steer straight

d) Accelerate to maintain control of the vehicle

Answer: c) Ease off the accelerator and steer straight

243. Question: What does a white rectangular sign with red lettering indicate?

a) Speed limit ahead

b) Construction zone ahead

c) No stopping zone

d) Wrong way sign

Answer: d) Wrong way sign

244. Question: What should you do if you are driving and your vehicle's headlights suddenly go out?

a) Continue driving at a slower speed

b) Turn on your emergency hazard lights and proceed cautiously

c) Pull off the road as soon as it is safe to do so

d) Use your high beams until you reach a safe location

Answer: c) Pull off the road as soon as it is safe to do so

245. Question: What does a solid white line on the roadway indicate?

a) Lane change is permitted

b) Passing is allowed

c) Lane change is prohibited

d) Pedestrian crossing ahead

Answer: c) Lane change is prohibited

246. Question: What should you do if you are driving and your vehicle's accelerator becomes stuck?

a) Shift into neutral and safely move to the side of the road

b) Turn off the ignition to shut off the engine

c) Apply the parking brake to slow down and stop the vehicle

d) Quickly pump the accelerator to loosen it

Answer: a) Shift into neutral and safely move to the side of the road

247. Question: What does a green circular sign indicate?

a) Stop and wait for the signal to turn green

b) Proceed with caution

c) Make a protected turn in the direction of the arrow

d) Yield to oncoming traffic

Answer: b) Proceed with caution

248. Question: What should you do if you are driving and a dust storm reduces visibility?

a) Turn on your high-beam headlights for better visibility

b) Pull off the road and park until the dust storm passes

c) Increase your speed to get through the dust storm quickly

d) Keep driving and honk your horn to alert other drivers

Answer: b) Pull off the road and park until the dust storm passes

249. Question: What does a yellow rectangular sign with black lettering indicate?

a) Speed limit ahead

b) School zone ahead

c) No parking zone

d) Stop sign ahead

Answer: a) Speed limit ahead

250. Question: What should you do if you are driving and your vehicle's brakes fail?

a) Pump the brakes rapidly to regain pressure

b) Shift into a lower gear to slow down the vehicle

c) Use the emergency/parking brake to gradually stop the vehicle

d) Steer off the road and into a soft surface to stop the vehicle

Answer: c) Use the emergency/parking brake to gradually stop the vehicle

251. Question: What does a white rectangular sign with

a black arrow pointing downward indicate?

a) Steep downhill grade ahead

b) Merge with traffic from the right

c) One-way traffic only

d) Exit ramp ahead

Answer: a) Steep downhill grade ahead

252. Question: What should you do when approaching a railroad crossing with flashing red lights and a lowered gate?

a) Stop at least 15 feet away from the railroad tracks

b) Slow down and proceed with caution if no train is visible

c) Proceed over the railroad tracks quickly to avoid delay

d) Change lanes and drive around the lowered gate

Answer: a) Stop at least 15 feet away from the railroad tracks

253. Question: What does a solid yellow line on the roadway indicate?

a) Passing is allowed

b) Lane change is prohibited

c) No stopping zone

d) Pedestrian crossing ahead

Answer: b) Lane change is prohibited

254. Question: What should you do if you are driving and encounter a funeral procession?

a) Honk your horn to express condolences

b) Follow the directions of the lead vehicle in the procession

c) Pass the procession quickly to avoid delay

d) Ignore the procession and continue driving

Answer: b) Follow the directions of the lead vehicle in the procession

255. Question: What does a red octagonal sign indicate?

a) Yield the right-of-way

b) Stop and wait for the signal to turn green

c) No passing zone

d) Merge with traffic from the right

Answer: b) Stop and wait for the signal to turn green

256. Question: What should you do if you are driving and a tire blows out?

a) Slam on the brakes to regain control

b) Steer in the opposite direction of the blowout

c) Ease off the accelerator and steer straight

d) Accelerate to maintain control of the vehicle

Answer: c) Ease off the accelerator and steer straight

257. Question: What does a blue circular sign indicate?

a) Motorist services ahead

b) Construction zone ahead

c) No parking zone

d) School zone ahead

Answer: a) Motorist services ahead

258. Question: What should you do if you are driving and encounter a bicyclist on the road?

a) Honk your horn to alert the bicyclist of your presence

b) Pass the bicyclist closely to save time

c) Slow down and give the bicyclist at least 3 feet of space

d) Speed up to get past the bicyclist quickly

Answer: c) Slow down and give the bicyclist at least 3 feet of space

259. Question: What does a red triangular sign with a white exclamation mark inside indicate?

a) Yield ahead

b) No passing zone

c) Warning of a potential hazard ahead

d) School zone ahead

Answer: c) Warning of a potential hazard ahead

260. Question: What should you do if you are driving and your vehicle's headlights suddenly go out?

a) Continue driving at a slower speed

b) Turn on your emergency hazard lights and proceed cautiously

c) Pull off the road as soon as it is safe to do so

d) Use your high beams until you reach a safe location

Answer: c) Pull off the road as soon as it is safe to do so

261. Question: What does a yellow diamond-shaped sign with black symbols of a person and a bicycle indicate?

a) Bicycle parking area ahead

b) Bicycles prohibited in the area

c) Shared lane with bicycles ahead

d) Bicycles must yield to pedestrians ahead

Answer: c) Shared lane with bicycles ahead

262. Question: What should you do if you are driving and your vehicle starts to skid?

a) Turn the steering wheel in the direction of the skid

b) Slam on the brakes to regain control

c) Accelerate to correct the skid

d) Ease off the accelerator and steer in the direction you want to go

Answer: d) Ease off the accelerator and steer in the direction you want to go

263. Question: What does a white rectangular sign with red lettering indicate?

a) Speed limit ahead

b) Construction zone ahead

c) No stopping zone

d) Wrong way sign

Answer: d) Wrong way sign

264. Question: What should you do if you are driving and encounter a flashing yellow traffic signal?

a) Come to a complete stop and wait for the signal to turn green

b) Slow down and proceed with caution

c) Yield the right-of-way to oncoming traffic

d) Speed up to clear the intersection quickly

Answer: b) Slow down and proceed with caution

265. Question: What does a solid white line on the roadway indicate?

a) Lane change is permitted

b) Passing is allowed

c) Lane change is prohibited

d) Pedestrian crossing ahead

Answer: c) Lane change is prohibited

266. Question: What should you do if you are driving and your vehicle's accelerator becomes stuck?

a) Shift into neutral and safely move to the side of the road

b) Turn off the ignition to shut off the engine

c) Apply the parking brake to slow down and stop the vehicle

d) Quickly pump the accelerator to loosen it

Answer: a) Shift into neutral and safely move to the side of the road

267. Question: What does a green circular sign indicate?

a) Stop and wait for the signal to turn green

b) Proceed with caution

c) Make a protected turn in the direction of the arrow

d) Yield to oncoming traffic

Answer: b) Proceed with caution

268. Question: What should you do if you are driving and encounter a flashing red traffic signal?

a) Come to a complete stop and wait for the signal to turn green

b) Slow down and proceed with caution

c) Yield the right-of-way to oncoming traffic

d) Speed up to clear the intersection quickly

Answer: a) Come to a complete stop and wait for the signal to turn green

269. Question: What does a yellow rectangular sign with black lettering indicate?

a) Speed limit ahead

b) School zone ahead

c) No parking zone

d) Stop sign ahead

Answer: a) Speed limit ahead

270. Question: What should you do if you are driving and your vehicle's brakes fail?

a) Pump the brakes rapidly to regain pressure

b) Shift into a lower gear to slow down the vehicle

c) Use the emergency/parking brake to gradually stop the vehicle

d) Steer off the road and into a soft surface to stop the vehicle

Answer: c) Use the emergency/parking brake to gradually stop the vehicle

271. Question: What does a solid yellow line alongside a broken yellow line on the roadway indicate?

a) Passing is allowed on the side with the broken yellow line

b) Passing is allowed on the side with the solid yellow line

c) No passing is allowed on either side

d) Passing is allowed on both sides

Answer: a) Passing is allowed on the side with the broken yellow line

272. Question: What should you do if you are driving and your vehicle's accelerator becomes stuck?

a) Shift into neutral and safely move to the side of the road

b) Turn off the ignition to shut off the engine

c) Apply the parking brake to slow down and stop the vehicle

d) Quickly pump the accelerator to loosen it

Answer: a) Shift into neutral and safely move to the side of the road

273. Question: What does a white rectangular sign with a red circle and a diagonal line indicate?

a) No stopping zone

b) No parking zone

c) Do not enter

d) No U-turn allowed

Answer: c) Do not enter

274. Question: When should you use your vehicle's high beam headlights?

a) In foggy conditions to improve visibility

b) When driving in well-lit urban areas

c) When following another vehicle closely

d) On dark roads or when there are no oncoming vehicles

Answer: d) On dark roads or when there are no oncoming vehicles

275. Question: What does a yellow circular sign with a black arrow and the word "DETOUR" indicate?

a) Lane ends, merge to the left

b) Road work ahead, follow the detour route

c) One-way traffic only

d) Pedestrian crossing ahead

Answer: b) Road work ahead, follow the detour route

276. Question: What should you do if you approach a curve and there is a vehicle approaching from the opposite direction?

a) Slow down and move as far to the right as possible

b) Speed up to pass the vehicle before the curve

c) Honk your horn to alert the other driver

d) Maintain your speed and position in your lane

Answer: a) Slow down and move as far to the right as possible

277. Question: What does a white rectangular sign with black lettering and a black border indicate?

a) School zone ahead

b) No passing zone

c) Stop sign ahead

d) Construction zone ahead

Answer: c) Stop sign ahead

278. Question: What should you do if you are driving and your vehicle's headlights suddenly go out?

a) Continue driving at a slower speed

b) Turn on your emergency hazard lights and proceed cautiously

c) Pull off the road as soon as it is safe to do so

d) Use your high beams until you reach a safe location

Answer: c) Pull off the road as soon as it is safe to do so

279. Question: What does a green rectangular sign indicate?

a) Destination guidance

b) Construction zone ahead

c) No parking zone

d) Hospital ahead

Answer: a) Destination guidance

280. Question: What should you do if you are driving and your vehicle's brakes fail?

a) Pump the brakes rapidly to regain pressure

b) Shift into a lower gear to slow down the vehicle

c) Use the emergency/parking brake to gradually stop the vehicle

d) Steer off the road and into a soft surface to stop the vehicle

Answer: c) Use the emergency/parking brake to gradually stop the vehicle

281. Question: What does a red triangular sign with a white border indicate?

a) Yield right-of-way

b) Stop ahead

c) Merge ahead

d) No passing zone

Answer: a) Yield right-of-way

282. Question: What should you do if you approach a railroad crossing with flashing red lights and a lowered crossing gate?

a) Stop and wait for the train to pass

b) Slow down and proceed with caution

c) Speed up to clear the tracks quickly

d) Change lanes and bypass the crossing

Answer: a) Stop and wait for the train to pass

283. Question: What does a blue circular sign with a white picture of a car and an arrow indicate?

a) Parking allowed

b) One-way street

c) Authorized vehicles only

d) Highway exit ahead

Answer: d) Highway exit ahead

284. Question: What should you do if you are driving and your vehicle's tire blows out?

a) Immediately apply the brakes to slow down the vehicle

b) Steer off the road and into a safe area

c) Grip the steering wheel firmly and maintain a straight course

d) Pump the brakes rapidly to regain control

Answer: c) Grip the steering wheel firmly and maintain a straight course

285. Question: What does a yellow diamond-shaped sign with black symbols of a truck and a downward arrow indicate?

a) Truck loading zone ahead

b) Trucks must use lower gear on downhill grades

c) Trucks must yield to pedestrians ahead

d) Truck weigh station ahead

Answer: b) Trucks must use lower gear on downhill grades

286. Question: What should you do if you approach a pedestrian crossing the street within a marked crosswalk?

a) Slow down and proceed with caution

b) Stop and wait for the pedestrian to cross

c) Honk your horn to alert the pedestrian

d) Drive around the pedestrian

Answer: b) Stop and wait for the pedestrian to cross

287. Question: What does a white rectangular sign with a red circle and a line through it indicate?

a) Speed limit ahead

b) No parking zone

c) No passing zone

d) No U-turn allowed

Answer: c) No passing zone

288. Question: What should you do if you are driving and there is heavy rain, reducing visibility significantly?

a) Turn on your high beam headlights for better visibility

b) Increase your speed to reach your destination quickly

c) Slow down, use your low beam headlights, and leave extra space between vehicles

d) Pull over to the side of the road until the rain subsides

Answer: c) Slow down, use your low beam headlights, and leave extra space between vehicles

289. Question: What does a yellow rectangular sign with black lettering and a black arrow indicate?

a) School zone ahead

b) No passing zone

c) Yield right-of-way

d) Detour ahead

Answer: d) Detour ahead

290. Question: What should you do if you are driving and encounter a bicyclist on the road?

a) Honk your horn to alert the bicyclist

b) Pass the bicyclist as closely as possible

c) Slow down and give the bicyclist plenty of space

d) Ignore the bicyclist and continue driving

Answer: c) Slow down and give the bicyclist plenty of space

291. Question: What does a red circular sign with a white horizontal line indicate?

a) Stop sign ahead

b) Railroad crossing ahead

c) Yield right-of-way

d) Do not enter

Answer: d) Do not enter

292. Question: When should you use your vehicle's hazard lights?

a) When driving in heavy rain or fog

b) When parking illegally for a short period

c) When you need to make a quick stop

d) When driving at night on a well-lit road

Answer: a) When driving in heavy rain or fog

293. Question: What does a white rectangular sign with a red circle and a white number indicate?

a) Speed limit for the area

b) Distance to the next town

c) Exit number for a highway

d) Mileage marker for the road

Answer: a) Speed limit for the area

294. Question: What should you do if you are driving and your vehicle's engine starts to overheat?

a) Turn on the air conditioning to cool down the engine

b) Drive at a higher speed to increase airflow to the engine

c) Pull over and turn off the engine to let it cool down

d) Continuously rev the engine to increase coolant circulation

Answer: c) Pull over and turn off the engine to let it cool down

295. Question: What does a yellow diamond-shaped sign with black symbols of two arrows pointing in opposite directions indicate?

a) Two-way traffic ahead

b) Divided highway ends

c) Merge with oncoming traffic

d) Roadway narrowing ahead

Answer: b) Divided highway ends

296. Question: What should you do if you are driving and a tire blows out?

a) Brake suddenly to bring the vehicle to a stop

b) Steer off the road and into a safe area

c) Immediately pull the emergency brake

d) Keep a firm grip on the steering wheel and gradually slow down

Answer: d) Keep a firm grip on the steering wheel and gradually slow down

297. Question: What does a white rectangular sign with a green bicycle symbol indicate?

a) Bicycle parking area

b) Bicycle lane ahead

c) Bicycle crossing ahead

d) Share the road with bicycles

Answer: b) Bicycle lane ahead

298. Question: What should you do if you are driving and your vehicle's brakes feel spongy or unresponsive?

a) Pump the brakes several times to restore pressure

b) Shift into a lower gear to slow down the vehicle

c) Continuously apply the brakes until they respond

d) Immediately pull over and have your brakes inspected

Answer: d) Immediately pull over and have your brakes inspected

299. Question: What does a yellow rectangular sign with black lettering and a black picture of a person walking indicate?

a) School zone ahead

b) Crosswalk ahead

c) Pedestrian crossing ahead

d) Watch for children playing

Answer: c) Pedestrian crossing ahead

300. Question: What should you do if you are driving and your vehicle's accelerator becomes stuck?

a) Turn off the ignition to shut off the engine

b) Apply the parking brake to slow down and stop the vehicle

c) Shift into neutral and safely move to the side of the road

d) Quickly pump the accelerator to loosen it

Answer: c) Shift into neutral and safely move to the side of the road

301. Question: What does a yellow triangular sign with a black exclamation mark indicate?

a) Construction zone ahead

b) Road work zone ahead

c) Warning sign ahead

d) School zone ahead

Answer: c) Warning sign ahead

302. Question: What should you do if you encounter a large animal crossing the road?

a) Slow down or stop if necessary, and allow the animal to cross safely

b) Honk your horn to scare the animal away

c) Swerve around the animal to avoid hitting it

d) Speed up to get past the animal quickly

Answer: a) Slow down or stop if necessary, and allow the animal to cross safely

303. Question: What does a white rectangular sign with a green circle and a white bicycle symbol indicate?

a) Bicycle repair shop ahead

b) Bicycle race in progress

c) Bicycle route or path ahead

d) Share the road with bicycles

Answer: c) Bicycle route or path ahead

304. Question: What should you do if you are driving and your vehicle's headlights suddenly stop working?

a) Keep driving and use your high beams to see the road

b) Continue driving but reduce your speed significantly

c) Pull over to the side of the road and turn on your hazard lights

d) Activate your emergency lights and drive to the nearest mechanic

Answer: c) Pull over to the side of the road and turn on your hazard lights

305. Question: What does a red circular sign with a white line through it indicate?

a) No U-turn allowed

b) Stop sign ahead

c) No entry

d) No passing zone

Answer: c) No entry

306. Question: What should you do if you are driving and your vehicle's windshield wipers fail during heavy rain?

a) Increase your speed to reduce rain accumulation on the windshield

b) Use your hand to wipe the windshield manually

c) Slow down and pull over to the side of the road until the rain subsides

d) Activate the defroster and adjust the air conditioning to clear the windshield

Answer: c) Slow down and pull over to the side of the road until the rain subsides

307. Question: What does a green circular sign with a white arrow indicate?

a) Exit only

b) Intersection ahead

c) Hospital ahead

d) Roundabout ahead

Answer: d) Roundabout ahead

308. Question: What should you do if you are driving and your vehicle's steering becomes difficult?

a) Turn the steering wheel rapidly to regain control

b) Pull over and check the tires for damage

c) Slow down and use firm, steady pressure on the steering wheel

d) Activate the hazard lights and continue driving at a reduced speed

Answer: c) Slow down and use firm, steady pressure on the steering wheel

309. Question: What does a white rectangular sign with a black picture of a bicycle indicate?

a) Bicycle repair shop ahead

b) Bicycle lane ends

c) Bicycle parking area ahead

d) Share the road with bicycles

Answer: c) Bicycle parking area ahead

310. Question: What should you do if you are driving and your vehicle's accelerator pedal becomes stuck?

a) Turn off the ignition to shut off the engine

b) Apply the parking brake to slow down and stop the vehicle

c) Shift into neutral and safely move to the side of the road

d) Pump the accelerator

311. Question: What does a yellow circular sign with a black arrow and the word "Detour" indicate?

a) Road closed ahead

b) No left turn allowed

c) Detour route ahead

d) Merge with oncoming traffic

Answer: c) Detour route ahead

312. Question: What should you do if you are driving and your vehicle's brakes fail?

a) Shift into a lower gear and pump the brakes

b) Use the parking brake to slow down the vehicle

c) Steer off the road and into a safe area

d) Downshift and use the engine to slow down the vehicle

Answer: d) Downshift and use the engine to slow down the vehicle

313. Question: What does a yellow rectangular sign with two black diagonal arrows

pointing in opposite directions indicate?

a) Divided highway begins

b) No passing zone ends

c) Roadway narrows ahead

d) Two-way traffic ahead

Answer: c) Roadway narrows ahead

314. Question: What should you do if you are driving and encounter a flashing yellow traffic signal?

a) Stop and yield the right-of-way to oncoming traffic

b) Proceed with caution and yield to pedestrians

c) Come to a complete stop and wait for the signal to turn green

d) Treat it as a stop sign and come to a complete stop before proceeding

Answer: b) Proceed with caution and yield to pedestrians

315. Question: What does a red triangular sign with a

white exclamation mark indicate?

a) Construction zone ahead

b) Yield the right-of-way

c) Warning sign ahead

d) School zone ahead

Answer: c) Warning sign ahead

316. Question: What should you do if you are driving and a tire blows out?

a) Brake suddenly to bring the vehicle to a stop

b) Steer off the road and into a safe area

c) Immediately pull the emergency brake

d) Keep a firm grip on the steering wheel and gradually slow down

Answer: d) Keep a firm grip on the steering wheel and gradually slow down

317. Question: What does a green rectangular sign with a white bicycle symbol indicate?

a) Bicycle parking area

b) Bicycle lane ahead

c) Bicycle crossing ahead

d) Share the road with bicycles

Answer: b) Bicycle lane ahead

318. Question: What should you do if you are driving and your vehicle's brakes feel spongy or unresponsive?

a) Pump the brakes several times to restore pressure

b) Shift into a lower gear to slow down the vehicle

c) Continuously apply the brakes until they respond

d) Immediately pull over and have your brakes inspected

Answer: d) Immediately pull over and have your brakes inspected

319. Question: What does a white rectangular sign with a green circle and a white picture of a bicycle indicate?

a) Bicycle repair shop ahead

b) Bicycle race in progress

c) Bicycle route or path ahead

d) Share the road with bicycles

Answer: c) Bicycle route or path ahead

320. Question: What should you do if you are driving and your vehicle's accelerator becomes stuck?

a) Turn off the ignition to shut off the engine

b) Apply the parking brake to slow down and stop the vehicle

c) Shift into neutral and safely move to the side of the road

d) Quickly pump the accelerator to loosen it

Answer: c) Shift

321. Question: What does a red circular sign with a white horizontal line indicate?

a) Stop sign ahead

b) Railroad crossing ahead

c) Yield right-of-way

d) Do not enter

Answer: d) Do not enter

322. Question: When should you use your vehicle's hazard lights?

a) When driving in heavy rain or fog

b) When parking illegally for a short period

c) When you need to make a quick stop

d) When driving at night on a well-lit road

Answer: a) When driving in heavy rain or fog

323. Question: What does a white rectangular sign with a red circle and a white number indicate?

a) Speed limit for the area

b) Distance to the next town

c) Exit number for a highway

d) Mileage marker for the road

Answer: a) Speed limit for the area

324. Question: What should you do if you are driving and your vehicle's engine starts to overheat?

a) Turn on the air conditioning to cool down the engine

b) Drive at a higher speed to increase airflow to the engine

c) Pull over and turn off the engine to let it cool down

d) Continuously rev the engine to increase coolant circulation

Answer: c) Pull over and turn off the engine to let it cool down

325. Question: What does a yellow diamond-shaped sign with black symbols of two arrows pointing in opposite directions indicate?

a) Two-way traffic ahead

b) Divided highway ends

c) Merge with oncoming traffic

d) Roadway narrowing ahead

Answer: b) Divided highway ends

326. Question: What should you do if you are driving and a tire blows out?

a) Brake suddenly to bring the vehicle to a stop

b) Steer off the road and into a safe area

c) Immediately pull the emergency brake

d) Keep a firm grip on the steering wheel and gradually slow down

Answer: d) Keep a firm grip on the steering wheel and gradually slow down

327. Question: What does a white rectangular sign with a green bicycle symbol indicate?

a) Bicycle parking area

b) Bicycle lane ahead

c) Bicycle crossing ahead

d) Share the road with bicycles

Answer: b) Bicycle lane ahead

328. Question: What should you do if you are driving and your vehicle's brakes feel spongy or unresponsive?

a) Pump the brakes several times to restore pressure

b) Shift into a lower gear to slow down the vehicle

c) Continuously apply the brakes until they respond

d) Immediately pull over and have your brakes inspected

Answer: d) Immediately pull over and have your brakes inspected

329. Question: What does a yellow rectangular sign with black lettering and a black picture of a person walking indicate?

a) School zone ahead

b) Crosswalk ahead

c) Pedestrian crossing ahead

d) Watch for children playing

Answer: c) Pedestrian crossing ahead

330. Question: What should you do if you are driving and your vehicle's accelerator becomes stuck?

a) Turn off the ignition to shut off the engine

b) Apply the parking brake to slow down and stop the vehicle

c) Shift into neutral and safely move to the side of the road

d) Quickly pump the accelerator to loosen it

Answer: c) Shift into neutral and safely move to the side of the road

331. Question: What does a yellow circular sign with a black arrow and the word "One Way" indicate?

a) No entry allowed

b) Vehicles must go in the direction of the arrow

c) Vehicles must yield to oncoming traffic

d) Intersection ahead

Answer: b) Vehicles must go in the direction of the arrow

332. Question: When approaching a stopped school bus with its red lights flashing and stop sign extended, what should you do?

a) Slow down and proceed with caution

b) Pass the school bus carefully on the left side

c) Stop and remain stopped until the bus resumes motion

d) Honk to alert the bus driver

Answer: c) Stop and remain stopped until the bus resumes motion

333. Question: What does a white rectangular sign with a red octagon and the word "STOP" indicate?

a) Yield the right-of-way

b) Slow down and proceed with caution

c) Come to a complete stop and yield to cross traffic

d) Merge with oncoming traffic

Answer: c) Come to a complete stop and yield to cross traffic

334. Question: What does a green circular sign with a white picture of a bicycle indicate?

a) Bicycle lane ends

b) Share the road with bicycles

c) No bicycles allowed

d) Bicycle parking area ahead

Answer: b) Share the road with bicycles

335. Question: What should you do if you are driving and your vehicle's headlights suddenly go out?

a) Keep driving and use your high beams

b) Turn on the hazard lights and continue driving

c) Pull over to a safe area and check the headlights

d) Flash your high beams to warn other drivers

Answer: c) Pull over to a safe area and check the headlights

336. Question: What does a white rectangular sign with a black arrow curving to the right indicate?

a) Right turn only

b) Right curve ahead

c) No right turns allowed

d) Exit ramp ahead

Answer: b) Right curve ahead

337. Question: When parking uphill with a curb, which way should you turn your vehicle's front wheels?

a) Towards the curb

b) Away from the curb

c) Straight ahead

d) It doesn't matter

Answer: b) Away from the curb

338. Question: What does a yellow rectangular sign with a black picture of a deer indicate?

a) Wildlife crossing area

b) Hunting area ahead

c) Deer farm ahead

d) Watch for fallen rocks

Answer: a) Wildlife crossing area

339. Question: What should you do if you are driving and encounter a flashing red traffic signal?

a) Stop and yield the right-of-way to oncoming traffic

b) Proceed with caution and yield to pedestrians

c) Come to a complete stop and wait for the signal to turn green

d) Treat it as a stop sign and come to a complete stop before proceeding

Answer: a) Stop and yield the right-of-way to oncoming traffic

340. Question: What does a yellow rectangular sign with black lettering and a black picture of a truck indicate?

a) Truck stop ahead

b) Watch for trucks merging onto the highway

c) Truck weigh station ahead

d) Trucks prohibited on this road

Answer: c) Truck weigh station ahead

341. Question: What does a red triangular sign with a white exclamation mark indicate?

a) Construction zone ahead

b) Slow down and proceed with caution

c) Road work ahead

d) Warning sign ahead

Answer: d) Warning sign ahead

342. Question: What should you do if you are driving and a tire blows out?

a) Brake suddenly to bring the vehicle to a stop

b) Steer off the road and into a safe area

c) Immediately pull the emergency brake

d) Keep a firm grip on the steering wheel and gradually slow down

d) Quickly pump the accelerator to loosen it

Answer: d) Keep a firm grip on the steering wheel and gradually slow down

Answer: c) Shift into neutral and safely move to the side of the road

343. Question: What does a white rectangular sign with a black picture of a person running indicate?

a) Marathon ahead

b) Jogging path ahead

c) Watch for pedestrians

d) Crosswalk ahead

345. Question: What does a yellow rectangular sign with black lettering and a black picture of a truck indicate?

a) Truck stop ahead

b) Watch for trucks merging onto the highway

c) Truck weigh station ahead

d) Trucks prohibited on this road

Answer: c) Watch for pedestrians

344. Question: What should you do if you are driving and your vehicle's accelerator becomes stuck?

a) Turn off the ignition to shut off the engine

b) Apply the parking brake to slow down and stop the vehicle

c) Shift into neutral and safely move to the side of the road

Answer: c) Truck weigh station ahead

346. Question: What does a white rectangular sign with a red circle and a red line across a picture of a bicycle indicate?

a) No bicycles allowed

b) Bicycles must yield to pedestrians

c) Bicycles prohibited on this road

d) Bicycles must dismount and walk

Answer: a) No bicycles allowed

347. Question: What should you do if you are driving and a traffic signal is malfunctioning?

a) Treat it as a stop sign and come to a complete stop

b) Proceed through the intersection without stopping

c) Slow down and proceed with caution

d) Follow the instructions of a police officer present

Answer: a) Treat it as a stop sign and come to a complete stop

348. Question: What does a white rectangular sign with a black arrow pointing to the right indicate?

a) Right turn only

b) Right curve ahead

c) No right turns allowed

d) Exit ramp ahead

Answer: a) Right turn only

349. Question: What should you do if you are driving and your vehicle's brakes feel spongy or unresponsive?

a) Pump the brakes several times to restore pressure

b) Shift into a lower gear to slow down the vehicle

c) Continuously apply the brakes until they respond

d) Immediately pull over and have your brakes inspected

Answer: d) Immediately pull over and have your brakes inspected

350. Question: What does a yellow circular sign with a black arrow and the word "One Way" indicate?

a) No entry allowed

b) Vehicles must go in the direction of the arrow

c) Vehicles must yield to oncoming traffic

d) Intersection ahead

Answer: b) Vehicles must go in the direction of the arrow

351. Question: What does a red circular sign with a white horizontal line indicate?

a) No left turns allowed

b) No U-turns allowed

c) No right turns allowed

d) No turns allowed

Answer: d) No turns allowed

352. Question: What should you do if you approach a railroad crossing and the crossing gates are lowered?

a) Drive around the gates if no train is approaching

b) Stop at least 15 feet away from the tracks and wait for the gates to raise

c) Proceed with caution if there are no flashing lights or a train in sight

d) Speed up to quickly cross the tracks before the train arrives

Answer: b) Stop at least 15 feet away from the tracks and wait for the gates to raise

353. Question: What does a white rectangular sign with a black picture of a bicycle and an arrow pointing to the right indicate?

a) Right turn only for bicycles

b) Bicycle lane ends ahead

c) Bicycles must merge to the right

d) Bicycle crossing ahead

Answer: c) Bicycles must merge to the right

354. Question: When parking downhill with a curb, which way should you turn your vehicle's front wheels?

a) Towards the curb

b) Away from the curb

c) Straight ahead

d) It doesn't matter

Answer: a) Towards the curb

355. Question: What does a white rectangular sign with

a black picture of a car and a curved arrow pointing to the right indicate?

a) Right turn only

b) Right curve ahead

c) No right turns allowed

d) Exit ramp ahead

Answer: b) Right curve ahead

356. Question: What should you do if you are driving and your vehicle's gas pedal gets stuck?

a) Turn off the ignition to shut off the engine

b) Apply the parking brake to slow down and stop the vehicle

c) Shift into neutral and safely move to the side of the road

d) Quickly pump the gas pedal to loosen it

Answer: c) Shift into neutral and safely move to the side of the road

357. Question: What does a white rectangular sign with a black arrow pointing upwards indicate?

a) Hill ahead

b) Merge with oncoming traffic

c) One-way street ahead

d) Overhead clearance ahead

Answer: d) Overhead clearance ahead

358. Question: What should you do if you are driving and your vehicle starts to skid?

a) Steer in the opposite direction of the skid

b) Brake quickly to regain control

c) Accelerate to gain traction

d) Ease off the accelerator and steer in the direction of the skid

Answer: d) Ease off the accelerator and steer in the direction of the skid

359. Question: What does a yellow rectangular sign with a black picture of a truck tipping over indicate?

a) Watch for trucks merging onto the highway

b) Truck stop ahead

c) Steep downgrade for trucks ahead

d) Curvy road ahead, use caution

Answer: c) Steep downgrade for trucks ahead

360. Question: What should you do if you are driving and a tire blows out?

a) Brake suddenly to bring the vehicle to a stop

b) Steer off the road and into a safe area

c) Immediately pull the emergency brake

d) Keep a firm grip on the steering wheel and gradually slow down

361. Question: What does a green arrow signal indicate?

a) Proceed with caution

b) Stop and wait for the green light

c) You can safely turn in the direction of the arrow

d) You must yield to oncoming traffic

Answer: c) You can safely turn in the direction of the arrow

362. Question: When are you allowed to use your vehicle's high beam headlights?

a) When driving in foggy conditions

b) When driving in residential areas

c) When there are no other vehicles around

d) When driving on a well-lit highway

Answer: c) When there are no other vehicles around

363. Question: What should you do if you approach a yellow traffic signal?

a) Speed up to quickly cross the intersection

b) Stop if it is safe to do so

c) Continue through the intersection without stopping

d) Yield to pedestrians and proceed with caution

Answer: d) Yield to pedestrians and proceed with caution

364. Question: What does a blue circular sign with a white wheelchair symbol indicate?

a) Designated parking for persons with disabilities

b) Hospital ahead

c) Pedestrian crosswalk ahead

d) Emergency parking only

Answer: a) Designated parking for persons with disabilities

365. Question: What does a white rectangular sign with a red circle and diagonal line indicate?

a) No parking allowed

b) No stopping or standing allowed

c) No left turns allowed

d) No entry allowed

Answer: d) No entry allowed

366. Question: What should you do if you are being tailgated by another vehicle?

a) Increase your speed to create more distance

b) Tap your brakes to warn the driver behind you

c) Pull over to let the vehicle pass

d) Maintain your speed and avoid sudden braking

Answer: d) Maintain your speed and avoid sudden braking

367. Question: What does a yellow rectangular sign with black letters "RR" indicate?

a) Railroad crossing ahead

b) Right turn only

c) Rest area ahead

d) Roadwork ahead

Answer: a) Railroad crossing ahead

368. Question: When parking uphill with a curb, which way should you turn

your vehicle's front wheels?

a) Towards the curb

b) Away from the curb

c) Straight ahead

d) It doesn't matter

Answer: b) Away from the curb

369. Question: What does a yellow diamond-shaped sign with a black symbol of a person walking indicate?

a) School zone ahead

b) Pedestrian crossing ahead

c) Crosswalk ahead

d) Sidewalk closed ahead

Answer: b) Pedestrian crossing ahead

370. Question: What should you do if you approach a flashing red traffic signal?

a) Come to a complete stop and proceed when safe

b) Slow down and proceed with caution

c) Treat it as a yield sign

d) Ignore the signal and continue driving

Answer: a) Come to a complete stop and proceed when safe

371. Question: When should you use your vehicle's hazard lights?

a) When driving in heavy rain

b) When parking illegally

c) When driving in heavy traffic

d) When experiencing a vehicle breakdown or emergency situation

Answer: d) When experiencing a vehicle breakdown or emergency situation

372. Question: What does a yellow rectangular sign with a black arrow pointing to the right indicate?

a) Right turn only

b) Merge with oncoming traffic

c) One-way street ahead

d) Exit ramp ahead

Answer: a) Right turn only

373. Question: What should you do if you encounter a large animal crossing the road?

a) Honk your horn and speed up to scare the animal away

b) Swerve to avoid the animal

c) Slow down or stop to allow the animal to safely cross

d) Flash your headlights to signal the animal to move

Answer: c) Slow down or stop to allow the animal to safely cross

374. Question: What does a white rectangular sign with a black arrow pointing upwards indicate?

a) Hill ahead

b) Merge with oncoming traffic

c) One-way street ahead

d) Overhead clearance ahead

Answer: d) Overhead clearance ahead

375. Question: What should you do if you are driving and encounter a funeral procession with its headlights on?

a) Follow closely behind the procession to maintain the flow of traffic

b) Yield the right-of-way and allow the procession to proceed uninterrupted

c) Pass the procession on the left side when it is safe to do so

d) Honk your horn to show respect for the deceased

Answer: b) Yield the right-of-way and allow the procession to proceed uninterrupted

376. Question: What does a red octagonal sign with white letters "STOP" indicate?

a) Proceed with caution

b) Slow down and prepare to stop

c) Stop and yield the right-of-way

d) Merge with oncoming traffic

Answer: c) Stop and yield the right-of-way

377. Question: What should you do if you miss your intended exit on a highway?

a) Continue driving and exit at the next available exit

b) Stop on the shoulder and reverse back to the missed exit

c) Make a U-turn and go back to the missed exit

d) Back up on the highway to reach the missed exit

Answer: a) Continue driving and exit at the next available exit

378. Question: What does a white rectangular sign with a black symbol of a bicycle and an arrow pointing to the right indicate?

a) Right turn only for bicycles

b) Bicycle lane ends ahead

c) Bicycles must merge to the right

d) Bicycle crossing ahead

Answer: c) Bicycles must merge to the right

379. Question: What should you do when approaching a yield sign?

a) Come to a complete stop

b) Slow down and proceed with caution

c) Increase your speed and merge with traffic

d) Ignore the sign and continue driving

Answer: b) Slow down and proceed with caution

380. Question: What does a yellow circular sign with a black symbol of a pedestrian crossing indicate?

a) No pedestrians allowed

b) Pedestrian crossing ahead

c) Yield to pedestrians

d) Pedestrian zone ahead

Answer: b) Pedestrian crossing ahead

381. Question: When is it legal to pass another vehicle on the right?

a) When the vehicle ahead is turning left

b) When the vehicle ahead is driving below the speed limit

c) When there is a designated right-turn lane

d) When the roadway has two or more lanes in each direction

Answer: d) When the roadway has two or more lanes in each direction

382. Question: What should you do if you encounter a flashing red traffic signal?

a) Come to a complete stop and proceed when it is safe

b) Slow down and proceed with caution

c) Treat it as a yield sign and proceed without stopping

d) Ignore the signal and continue driving

Answer: a) Come to a complete stop and proceed when it is safe

383. Question: What does a green arrow signal mean?

a) Proceed with caution

b) Prepare to stop

c) Yield to oncoming traffic

d) You may proceed in the direction of the arrow

Answer: d) You may proceed in the direction of the arrow

384. Question: What does a double solid yellow line indicate?

a) No passing in either direction

b) Passing is allowed on the right side only

c) Passing is allowed on the left side only

d) Passing is allowed in both directions

Answer: a) No passing in either direction

385. Question: What should you do if you are approaching a steady red traffic signal?

a) Slow down and proceed with caution

b) Come to a complete stop and wait for the signal to turn green

c) Stop only if there is cross traffic

d) Stop only if there is a police officer present

Answer: b) Come to a complete stop and wait for the signal to turn green

386. Question: When should you use your vehicle's high-beam headlights?

a) In foggy or misty conditions

b) When driving in heavy traffic

c) When approaching oncoming traffic

d) When driving on poorly lit roads

Answer: d) When driving on poorly lit roads

387. Question: What does a yellow diamond-shaped sign with black symbols of a deer indicate?

a) Wildlife crossing ahead

b) Deer hunting area

c) Deer feeding zone

d) Deer prohibited

Answer: a) Wildlife crossing ahead

388. Question: What does a yellow circular sign with a black symbol of a train indicate?

a) Train crossing ahead

b) No trains allowed

c) Yield to trains

d) Train station ahead

Answer: a) Train crossing ahead

389. Question: What should you do when you encounter a flashing yellow traffic signal?

a) Stop and yield the right-of-way

b) Proceed with caution

c) Speed up to clear the intersection quickly

d) Treat it as a stop sign and come to a complete stop

Answer: b) Proceed with caution

390. Question: What does a white rectangular sign with black letters "EXIT" indicate?

a) No exit ahead

b) Freeway entrance ahead

c) Exit ramp ahead

d) One-way street ahead

Answer: c) Exit ramp ahead

391. Question: When should you use your vehicle's hazard lights?

a) When driving in heavy traffic

b) When you want to warn other drivers of a road hazard

c) When you want to pass another vehicle

d) When you are driving at night

Answer: b) When you want to warn other drivers of a road hazard

392. Question: What does a white diamond-shaped sign with black symbols of a bicycle indicate?

a) Bicycle lane ahead

b) Bicycles prohibited

c) Share the road with bicycles

d) Bicycle rental area

Answer: c) Share the road with bicycles

393. Question: What is the purpose of a rumble strip on the roadway?

a) To guide drivers through curves

b) To alert drivers when they drift out of their lane

c) To indicate a pedestrian crossing area

d) To mark the entrance of a school zone

Answer: b) To alert drivers when they drift out of their lane

394. Question: What does a solid white line at the edge of the roadway indicate?

a) No passing in either direction

b) Passing is allowed on the right side only

c) Passing is allowed on the left side only

d) Passing is allowed in both directions

Answer: b) Passing is allowed on the right side only

395. Question: What should you do if your vehicle's accelerator pedal becomes stuck?

a) Pump the brakes to release the accelerator

b) Turn off the ignition to shut down the engine

c) Shift into neutral and gradually brake to a stop

d) Use your hand to lift the accelerator pedal

Answer: c) Shift into neutral and gradually brake to a stop

396. Question: When should you yield the right-of-way to pedestrians at a crosswalk?

a) Only if the pedestrian is already in the crosswalk

b) Only if the pedestrian is using a designated crosswalk

c) At all times, regardless of the location or type of crosswalk

d) Only if the pedestrian signals for you to stop

Answer: c) At all times, regardless of the location or type of crosswalk

397. Question: What is the purpose of a traffic circle or roundabout?

a) To slow down traffic and improve safety

b) To allow pedestrians to cross the road safely

c) To provide a designated area for parking

d) To allow vehicles to merge onto a highway

Answer: a) To slow down traffic and improve safety

398. Question: What should you do if you miss your intended highway exit?

a) Continue driving and take the next available exit

b) Stop and reverse on the highway to reach the missed exit

c) Pull over to the shoulder and wait for assistance

d) Make a U-turn on the highway to go back to the missed exit

Answer: a) Continue driving and take the next available exit

399. Question: When parking uphill with a curb, which way should you turn your front wheels?

a) Away from the curb

b) Towards the curb

c) It doesn't matter which way you turn the wheels

d) Parallel to the curb

Answer: a) Away from the curb

400. Question: What does a white rectangular sign with black symbols of a person in a wheelchair indicate?

a) Handicapped parking zone

b) Wheelchair rental area

c) Accessible pedestrian crossing

d) No pedestrians allowed

Answer: c) Accessible pedestrian crossing

401. Question: What does a red traffic sign with a white horizontal line indicate?

a) No parking zone

b) Stop ahead

c) Railroad crossing ahead

d) Construction zone ahead

Answer: b) Stop ahead

402. Question: When can you legally pass a vehicle on the right side?

a) When the vehicle is making a left turn

b) When there is a marked passing lane on the right

c) When the vehicle ahead is moving too slowly

d) When the vehicle is stopped at a red light

Answer: b) When there is a marked passing lane on the right

403. Question: What does a flashing yellow traffic signal indicate?

a) Stop and wait for the light to turn green

b) Proceed with caution

c) Slow down and yield to oncoming traffic

d) Come to a complete stop and yield the right-of-way

Answer: b) Proceed with caution

404. Question: What is the purpose of a speed limit sign?

a) To indicate the minimum speed limit on the road

b) To indicate the recommended speed for the road

c) To indicate the maximum speed allowed on the road

d) To indicate the average speed of vehicles on the road

Answer: c) To indicate the maximum speed allowed on the road

405. Question: When should you use your vehicle's high beam headlights?

a) When driving in fog or heavy rain

b) When driving in well-lit urban areas

c) When following another vehicle at a safe distance

d) When driving in dark or poorly lit areas

Answer: d) When driving in dark or poorly lit areas

406. Question: What does a green arrow signal mean?

a) Yield to oncoming traffic

b) Stop and do not proceed

c) Proceed in the direction of the arrow if safe

d) Prepare to make a left turn

Answer: c) Proceed in the direction of the arrow if safe

407. Question: What should you do when approaching a school bus with flashing red lights and an extended stop sign arm?

a) Proceed with caution and pass the bus if there are no children crossing

b) Slow down and prepare to stop until the lights stop flashing

c) Change lanes and continue driving at the same speed

d) Honk your horn to alert the bus driver

Answer: b) Slow down and prepare to stop until the lights stop flashing

408. Question: What should you do if you encounter a large truck or bus making a wide turn?

a) Speed up and pass the vehicle on the left side

b) Slow down and allow the vehicle to complete its turn

c) Drive alongside the vehicle to provide assistance

d) Honk your horn to alert the driver of your presence

Answer: b) Slow down and allow the vehicle to complete its turn

409. Question: When can you legally make a U-turn at an intersection?

a) When there is a "No U-turn" sign posted

b) When there is no oncoming traffic and it is safe to do so

c) When the traffic light is red

d) When there is a police officer directing traffic

Answer: b) When there is no oncoming traffic and it is safe to do so

410. Question: What does a blue circular sign with a white "H" symbol indicate?

a) Hospital ahead

b) Handicapped parking zone

c) Highway exit ahead

d) Hazardous material storage facility

Answer: a) Hospital ahead

That concludes the practice questions. Good luck with your continued preparations for the California DMV exam!

Made in the USA
Las Vegas, NV
18 November 2023

81120751R00125